D0305958

CAPTAIN'S DIARY
1989–1991

CAPTAIN'S DIARY 1989–1991

Will Carling

Chatto & Windus
LONDON

TO MY FAMILY

Published in 1991 by
Chatto & Windus Ltd
20 Vauxhall Bridge Road
London SW1V 2SA

All rights reserved. No part of this publi-
cation may be reproduced, stored in a
retrieval system, or transmitted in any form,
or by any means, electronic, mechanical,
photocopying, recording or otherwise, without the prior permission of the publisher.

A CIP catalogue record for his book is
available from the British Library.

ISBN 0 7011 3652 9

Copyright © Will Carling 1991

Will Carling has asserted his right to be identified
as the author of this work

Phototypeset by Intype, London
Printed in Great Britain by
Mackays

TO MY FAMILY

CONTENTS

LIST OF ILLUSTRATIONS

PICTURE CREDITS

Section One

Plate 2: Simon Bruty/Allsport; plates 14, 15, 16: David Cannon/Allsport; plates 3, 5, 6, 7, 9, 10, 11, 12, 17, 18, 20, 21: Russell Cheyne/Allsport; plate 13: Colin Elsey/ Colorsport; plate 19: V. R. Grubicy/Allsport; plates 4, 8: M. Leech/Colorsport.

Section Two

Plate 12: Howard Boylan/Allsport; plate 15: Simon Bruty/ Allsport; plates 1, 4, 5, 8, 11, 14: Russell Cheyne/Allsport; plates 3, 17: Andrew Cowie/Colorsport; plates 2, 6, 10, 13: Colin Elsey/Colorsport; plate 9: Stuart MacFarlane/ Colorsport; plate 19: Dan Smith/Allsport; plates 7, 16, 18: Billy Stickland/Allsport.

ACKNOWLEDGEMENTS

The author and publishers wish to thank the following for permission to reproduce photographs: the author's family; Simon Bruty, Russell Cheyne, David Cannon, V. R. Grubicy, Billy Stickland, Howard Boylan and Dan Smith, all of Allsport; M. Leech, Colin Elsey, Andrew Cowie and Stuart MacFarlane, all of Colorsport; Peter Lavery and Condé Nast Publications Ltd. The author and publishers wish to thank Paula Goodchild for her typing services.

The author would like to thank G. Cooke and R. Uttley for their advice and stabilising influences. And Alex, Jim and Henry.

PART ONE
1989–90

TUESDAY 10 SEPTEMBER 1989

We're at the outset of another international season, and I'm itching to go. I've a feeling this could be a big season for England; it's certainly going to be an important one for me personally. I've just suffered the only real setback of my rugby career so far, and I'm determined to put it behind me.

It was last autumn, at the age of twenty-two, that I was made England captain – the youngest ever. Moreover, the appointment was for three years, until the World Cup in October 1991. The England manager, Geoff Cooke, made the announcement at a team meeting. I was sitting at the front of the room, and most of the senior players were at the back, and although I was thrilled at what was happening, part of me was apprehensive. Would I get the acceptance of some of the older players? Or would they think me an upstart? I needn't have worried on that score. All the players were supportive as I found my feet in those early months. I led England through the 1988–89 Five Nations Championship, which we came close to winning, and it seemed that my international career was secure for the foreseeable future.

But for most of that first season in charge I was carrying an injury. A piece of bone had become detached from my shin – it was uncomfortable, and I knew I wasn't playing at my best. The only cure was a long rest from rugby. It was terribly disappointing, but I had no alternative except to make myself unavailable for the Lions tour of Australia the following summer.

It was a bad time to break down; to be sitting at home while other England players covered themselves with glory Down Under. Part of me couldn't help fearing that Geoff and Roger Uttley, the coach, might be regretting their decision to make me skipper. I was fairly confident that as long as I showed I could still thrive at international level Geoff would be happy to keep me as captain – but I couldn't prove that from the sidelines.

And then there were the pressmen. My appointment had generally been applauded as a brave decision for the future. But no sooner was I out injured than some seemed to assume I would never be back. However secure you think you are, it takes only a slight injury or loss of form for journalists and others to start casting around for the next captain. To make matters worse, competition was – and still is – very strong for the centre positions in the England team. Jeremy Guscott had replaced me for the match against Romania in April, and had scored three tries in his first international. He then went on to have an outstanding tour with the Lions, scoring that brilliant solo try in the Second Test that turned the series our way. Simon Halliday is still at his best, and it is going to be difficult to justify leaving him out, either.

Until my injury, I'd had nothing but good fortune in my rugby career. I didn't have to fight that hard for my England place and, once I got into the side, things went so well for me that within a year I was captain. In that sense, being out injured did me some good. I had the whole summer off, and discovered a different way of life. I suddenly had time to do things I couldn't do when I was playing. For the first time in years I could go shopping on a Saturday afternoon. I could go out to the theatre or to a party on Friday night. I could go away for weekends. I could let my fitness slip a notch or two without feeling guilty. And so, when I came back to rugby, it was with a shrewder sense of the sacrifices involved and why, for me, they were worth making. It was a bit of a struggle to get back to training seven days a week, and to recover my former levels of determination and dedication. But I think I now see my rugby career in a more mature way. I know now that it can be taken away at virtually any moment, by injury or loss of form, and I'm resolved to make the best of it while I have it.

I made my comeback playing for the Public School Wanderers in the Monte Carlo Sevens late last month. The Wanderers won the competition, but for me it was more important that my leg stood up to the rock-hard grounds. There were a lot of pressmen watching, and I think I convinced them that my injury was a thing of the past. That took some pressure off me. And a few days ago, I played for Harlequins against Bath, the toughest club fixture of them all. We lost, but I had no reaction from my leg. Geoff Cooke watched the game and saw my fitness for himself. So I hope I can say that the hiccup in my career is over.

SUNDAY 22 SEPTEMBER 1989

This week we had the first England selection meeting of the season, with Dick Best, Mike Slemen and John Elliott in attendance, as well as Geoff, Roger and myself. We laid out our objectives for the whole campaign. Dick and Mike were new to the selection committee, and we sorted out what they wanted to do and what Geoff wanted from them. I was glad to feel myself back in the thick of things on the management as well as on the playing side.

I'm the first England captain to have been given an official voice in selection, and this means I have to be careful. Players are naturally suspicious of committee men, and I have to make sure they realise I am a players' captain, that I will push their views even if it makes me unpopular with the management. I have no desire to be regarded as a yes-man, though I have to be wary also of seeming to press the claims of my own mates against others.

I spend a lot of time talking to the senior players, finding out from them about younger players, who might be on the verge of the England side. At selection meetings I try to speak for these senior players. It's easy for management to become alienated from the team and to be unaware of, say, internal misgivings about certain newcomers, or even about established players. I feel that I can make a useful contribution to selection in this way. Having said that, I must give credit to Geoff, Roger and John Elliott for the way they have completely overhauled attitudes within the England squad. The players now have the confidence which had been missing from English teams for a long time, mainly through bad selection. People will always question selectors' decisions, but the players now know that they will be given a fair chance. Geoff is not going to chop and change the team for every game; no one will be dropped on the basis of one indifferent performance. Newcomers to the England squad these days are always surprised to find how happy and friendly the atmosphere is, and that's largely down to Geoff.

At the selection meeting Geoff emphasised that this was not just the start of a new season, but the beginning of the build-up to the 1991 World Cup. Although we thought we had a good chance of winning England's first Grand Slam since 1980, Geoff is looking at the longer term. The game against Fiji on 4 November is, he feels, our last real chance to experiment before starting the preparations for the World Cup. There may be two Five Nations Tournaments to come before then, but that's not long when you are trying to build a secure squad. There have been high expectations of England since so many of our players figured in the successful Lions tour – a real feeling that this could be a Grand Slam year. Even so, Geoff feels that now is the time to start thinking about bringing young players into the squad.

We had a long, hard look at the England side from last year, and talked about what we could learn from the Lions tour. This had been the most successful touring side to go to the Southern Hemisphere in the Eighties, and they have brought back a lot of pride to British rugby. England supplied the bulk of the Lions pack, and Rob Andrew's influence at fly-half seemed to grow with every game. All the

7

English Lions learned a lot about their potential from the tour; they also learned about the opponents they'd be facing in the Five Nations Championship, especially the strong Scottish contingent: Finlay Calder, Derek White and John Jeffrey, David Sole, Gary Armstrong and Craig Chalmers, and the Hastings brothers. It looks as though the Scots will provide the toughest opposition for us this winter.

The Lions tour also confirmed some old faults. For example, we're still not as good as we could be at presenting the ball. But there's no doubt that we have the basis of a very good side. In the forwards we have a tenacious and skilful hooker in Brian Moore and a world-class back five. What we don't have are mobile props, and this was spoken about in depth at the selection meeting. Jeff Probyn, Paul Rendall and Gareth Chilcott are very experienced props and excellent in the set pieces. But we need to look for young men who can hold their own in the scrums, and also give something in the open field. And there don't seem to be any outstanding young props coming up. A few names were mentioned: Mullins, Sharp, Linnett, Mosses. Geoff, Dick and John were going to look closely at these players and invite them to the first squad sessions to see how they performed. My own feeling is that given the quality of the six other forwards, we ought to be able to incorporate two young props into the pack and bring them along for a year or so while they mature. The accent of forward play is moving away from big juggernauts towards a more athletic type, and the side of the Nineties will have props who can put in cover tackles, handle the ball, and run at pace. I am not belittling the older props, each of whom has done great things for England, but there comes a point when, if a game is evolving, you have to adapt accordingly.

We were very happy with the other six forwards, but we had to establish who would cover for them in case of injury or drastic loss of form. John Olver, my club captain, was a clear choice as the reserve hooker. We are lucky to have a lot of very talented back-row players, and it is going to be a tough choice between Peter Winterbottom and Andy Robinson on the open-side flank. We had to decide who would be the back-up at Number 8 for Dean Richards and Mike Teague: would it be Bath's Dave Egerton, or Dean Ryan, who had just moved from Saracens to Wasps, or Dave Thresher of Harlequins, who had done very well on the England B tour?

In the backs, we had to look closely at scrum-half. Should it be Steve Bates or Dewi Morris? And what about Richard Hill, who seems to have conquered his suspect temperament and is playing so well for Bath? Rob Andrew has no real competition at fly-half, but in the centre we have to choose between Jerry Guscott, Simon Halliday and myself. Rory Underwood is an obvious choice for one of the wings, but Chris Oti is out injured. Who should we have on the other wing? Mark Bailey seems the front-runner.

It was useful to have Dick Best and Mike Slemen there: two new views on the players available. I've always respected Dick who's one of the best coaches in the country. I'd never met Mike Slemen before this selection meeting, but as a player he'd been one of my heroes when I was at school. The atmosphere at the meeting was brisk and positive, and I left happy that we had a management with confidence and pride in the players.

SUNDAY 20 OCTOBER 1989

Today was the first England squad session of the season. There were forty players there – too many, I thought. Some of them were new, and some of those seemed to think they were only there to make up the numbers. With such a big group, it was hard for me to establish the kind of intimacy that the team had last year; I felt that I had to stand back and supervise the younger players. I wasn't too worried about the guys who had just come back from the Lions tour. It wouldn't have been reasonable to expect them to get worked up about a squad session like this, or to do anything more than go through the motions. But it was interesting to see how newer players like Andy Mullins, and Rory Underwood's brother Tony, and the young fly-half from Bristol, Paul Hull, coped with their first England session. I remember being petrified at mine. I felt that every pass I made was being scrutinised, and that if I dropped the ball just once my chance would be gone. Since I've got involved in the selection process I realise that although you do get an impression of the players from these sessions, you certainly don't base selection on them. Some of the new recruits looked the part; especially those who didn't seem put off if their position in the England team was occupied by a British Lion. They know we are taking a long view, with the autumn of 1991 as our final objective;

and the England B team is going to have an identity of its own, as a fostering ground for future internationals.

But there won't be that much scope for experiment in the next two years. If a player deserves an international place he must get one. But all the great international sides have been developed over several years. Great sides do not come about through the accidental combination of talented individuals. The obvious example is the All Blacks: one of the reasons they're so good is that from a very early age – through school, club and provincial level – all teams play exactly the same style of rugby. In England we don't have that consistency of style, although the league system may begin to bring it about. So when we come together at international level we are still trying to identify a style in which to play. I think that once this England team decides exactly what it wants to do, it could be a great side; that's why the game against Fiji is important, and why there isn't much room for manoeuvre in team selection. I want to keep the core of last year's side together, and if young players are to be introduced it must be for a reason. I don't see the point of throwing someone in for one match just 'to give him experience'. If we put in young props or wingers, it will be with the idea that they may start in the Five Nations Championship.

SUNDAY 27 OCTOBER 1989

We met at Twickenham today to select the team against Fiji. As I suspected, there was much debate about props. On the one hand, Paul Rendall and Jeff Probyn are easily the best set-piece props we have; their scrummaging and line-out play is world class. On the other hand, their fitness levels are not all they could be. There are fitter props around, and while these may not be ready for international rugby yet, there's a feeling around that Probyn and Rendall could do with the jolt of a little competition for their places. It's also important that young players throughout the country get the message that we want athletic forwards. We must learn from New Zealand, whose forwards all have agility and ball skills as well as tremendous power. So in come Andy Mullins, of Harlequins, and Moseley's Mark Linnett.

The core of last year's side have stayed together. Mike Teague and Dean Richards are injured and will be replaced by Micky Skinner and Dave Egerton respectively. The loss of Teague and Richards isn't as great a blow as it might have been, because Micky Skinner has been playing terrific rugby so far this season for Harlequins, and Dave Egerton is a player of international class, who has been unlucky to peak while Dean Richards has had a monopoly of the England Number 8 shirt. On the other flank we have opted for Peter Winterbottom over Andy Robinson. Andy had a great Five Nations last year, and went on the Lions tour, but Peter Winterbottom is bang in form and is known as a world-class player. Opponents really fear playing against him; you're always looking for him out of the corner of your eye, and if you see him coming you tend to unload the ball pretty quickly.

On paper it may have looked as if the pack has been disrupted, with the two new props and a completely new back row. But we still have the core of the Lions pack with Brian Moore, Wade Dooley and Paul Ackford, and the back row is arguably of Lions class. We have a very mobile pack which ought to produce good fast ball. At scrum-half we have recalled Richard Hill, whose club form has been irresistible. It was difficult to discard Steve Bates, who played well against Romania last spring, but Hill's pass is undoubtedly the fastest in the country, and that speed of service will give Rob Andrew the extra couple of yards he needs to release the back line and utilise our strength out wide. We've picked Jeremy Guscott in the centre, because he has shown such exceptional promise. He is a very talented player, though whether this game will give him the test he needs is doubtful; he'll certainly enjoy himself if it turns out as fast and loose as I expect. I've never played in the same side as him before, and it'll be interesting to see how we blend. It was a hard choice between Guscott and Simon Halliday – especially as Simon's a great friend of mine – but this is a game in which we can monitor players' progress, and I think we made the right decision. Rory Underwood and Mark Bailey are the wings. Simon Hodgkinson keeps his place at full back, because of his superb kicking; Jonathan Webb's form has slipped a bit at the moment.

I think, overall, we've made a bold selection. We've gone

for mobility and taken a few risks in certain areas which should produce some exciting rugby. It's not necessarily the team that will start the Five Nations, but the match should give a good indication of our prospects.

4 NOVEMBER 1989, TWICKENHAM

ENGLAND 58		FIJI 23	
Tries:	Underwood (5) Skinner Bailey Linnett Ackford Guscott	**Tries:**	Eranavula Teleni Rasari Savai
Conversions:	Hodgkinson (5) Andrew	**Conversions:**	Koroduadua (2)
		Penalty:	Koroduadua
Penalties:	Hodgkinson (2)		

Fourteen tries were scored in the match, but it was soured by Fijian frustration boiling over into dangerous play. Referee Brian Stirling sent off two Fijian threequarters, Vonolagi and Nadruku, for repeated head-high tackling.

Vonolagi had double reason to be unhappy, as his direct opponent Rory Underwood scored five tries down their wing. This equalled Daniel Lambert's record (set in 1907) for tries in one game by an England player, and it brought Underwood level with Cyril Lowe's career record of eighteen tries for England.

14

The control of their forwards was the key to England's supremacy; they were far too powerful for their inventive, athletic, but uncommitted opponents.

ENGLAND: S. D. Hodgkinson (Nottingham); R. Underwood (Leicester), J. C. Guscott (Bath), W. D. C. Carling (Harlequins) *(capt)*, M. D. Bailey (Wasps); C. R. Andrew (Wasps), R. J. Hill (Bath); M. S. Linnett (Moseley), B. C. Moore (Nottingham), A. R. Mullins (Harlequins), W. A. Dooley (Preston Grasshoppers), P. J. Ackford (Harlequins), M. G. Skinner (Harlequins), P. J. Winterbottom (Harlequins), D. W. Egerton (Bath)

Replacements: G. W. Rees (Nottingham) for Winterbottom; S. J. Halliday (Bath) for Bailey

FIJI: Naituilagilagi; Lovo, Eranavula, Nadruku, Vonolagi; Koroduadua, Vasuwulagi; Taga, Naiviliwasa, S. Naituku, Savai, Rasari, Matirawa, Dere, Teleni *(capt)*

Referee: B. W. Stirling (Ireland)

15

RORY AT SPEED

SUNDAY 5 NOVEMBER 1989

To score fifty points against any international side is an achievement. We did it against Romania in April, and now we've done it against Fiji. Perhaps neither of these sides are out of the top drawer, but Fiji take some beating – they ran France close in the last World Cup, remember. So I was happy to have come away with the team having scored so many tries.

This is really the first time since I joined the England squad that we have gone into a game with a definite aim in mind about the style we wanted to play and have actually seen it through. Perhaps it was disappointing that after a very good start we relaxed a bit. I take a certain amount of blame for that, for running a penalty that we could have kicked after ten minutes. That made everyone sit back a bit too much. Nevertheless, we did come back. We coped with their creativity and subdued them and we finished very strongly; the second-half performance was pretty satisfying, even if the sendings-off spoiled the atmosphere.

Most of the selection decisions were vindicated. The two new props worked very well. They looked mobile, they got their hands on the ball and drove, and they coped well with the set pieces. Micky Skinner had a superb game on the blind side of the back row.

On the debit side, we really must learn to concentrate

17

for the whole game; and perhaps our defence was a little lax. We let them through in the back row twice. We must maintain our hunger to keep our line intact.

The back play was much sharper than it had been in last year's Five Nations. We have to work on our support play, but our running and passing would have to be pretty good for Rory Underwood to score five tries, an England record.

Like the Romanian game, this was a hard match to prepare for mentally. We had nothing to gain; we were expected to win well. We managed that all night, but the game did reveal a few weaknesses. I and the senior players must think about these; we have to pinpoint areas to work on when the squad goes to Lanzarote in early January. Being honest about our deficiencies can only help improve our performance.

MONDAY 13 NOVEMBER 1989

Latest news on Mike Teague and Dean Richards: Mike's shoulder should be all right. The pain is coming from scar tissue in his ligaments, and that can be helped by ultrasound treatment and by slowly building up his weight training again. But Dean's situation is worse than we thought. He won't be fully fit until February at the earliest after a shoulder operation to realign his muscles, mend the cartilage and tighten the ligaments: quite a major operation, and a great blow to us. We have good back-up in Dave

BRIAN
MOORE !

Egerton and Mike Teague, but Dean is a unique presence, and his general influence, especially on the forwards, will be greatly missed. Dean is not only a vital player, but also the pack leader; now Brian Moore will take over that role. This may actually suit both players in the long run. Dean commands great respect among the players, but I don't think he likes really being the guy who has to do the talking. He's more relaxed when he can chip in here and there with the odd comment, and then drift back into the background

19

and get on with his own game. For Brian, on the other hand, talking is no problem. He is always in the thick of things, and I'm sure being pack leader will suit his temperament. Brian and I will have to work hard in the next few months to build up the necessary relationship of trust, understanding and friendship.

MONDAY 27 NOVEMBER 1989

More bad news – Chris Oti is not going to be fit in time to play for London in the Divisional Championship. His knee isn't right yet. He has had an operation which has strengthened the joint, and we've arranged some excellent physiotherapy for him, but he is still not happy about it in his own mind. He says himself that he's been playing for too long with a worry about his knee, and I think he is quite right to wait until he feels fully confident with it before he plays again.

TOP Terra Nova under-10s BOTTOM Meeting the Princess Royal before the Scotland match in 1989, my first Five Nations game as captain

ENGLAND *v* IRELAND 1990
TOP Jeremy Guscott surging clear to score and BOTTOM accepting my congratulations

FRANCE *v* ENGLAND 1990
Stretching out to score

ENGLAND *v* WALES 1990

A record victory
TOP LEFT Brian Moore, an inspirational pack leader TOP RIGHT Simon Halliday, a good friend and a versatile three-quarter BOTTOM Peter Winterbottom shows his new-found sleight of hand

TOP Breaking through Richie Collins' tackle and BOTTOM eluding Robert Jones and Mark Titley to squeeze in at the corner

SCOTLAND *v* ENGLAND 1990

Our Grand Slam hopes foundered on committed tackling like TOP LEFT Paul Burnell's on Paul Ackford and RIGHT John Jeffrey's on Richard Hill BOTTOM This time it was the Scots who celebrated

Rugby all over the world, 1990
CLOCKWISE, FROM TOP LEFT Sevens in Monte Carlo and Hong Kong; Fifteens in Italy and
Argentina

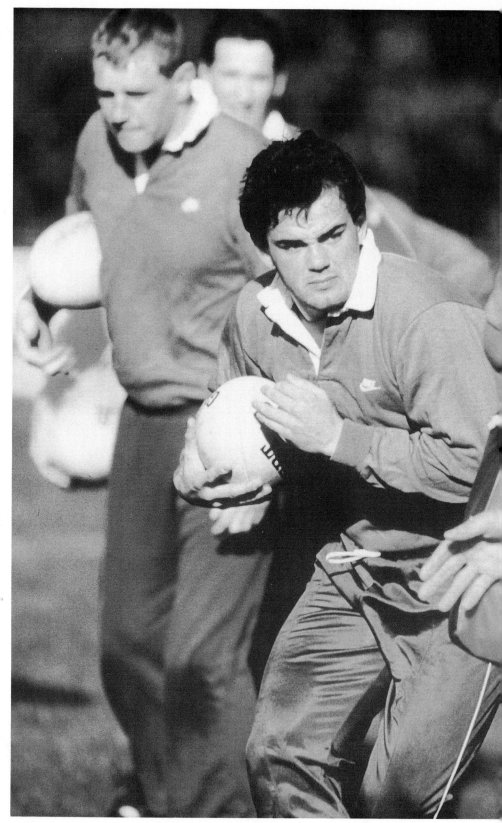

Back to the training ground; Dean Richards waits his turn

THURSDAY 30 NOVEMBER 1989

More damage. Mark Bailey has strained a hamstring against Bath and is probably now going to miss the Divisionals. This leaves us a little light on the wings for the time being, though I don't think his injury is all that serious. The doctor and the physio seem to think he will be fit by Christmas, which gives him plenty of time to get fit again before we go to Lanzarote.

FRIDAY 1 DECEMBER 1989

And more. Three-quarters are dropping like flies. Jerry Guscott will miss the first Divisional match, having taken a blow playing for the Barbarians against New Zealand last weekend. This is a bit worrying. The nose doesn't seem to be broken, and no one knows why he left the pitch. I spoke to Simon Halliday, his Divisional captain, and he doesn't know what the problem is. Guscott seems to have taken a

21

blow on the face and walked off. I hope he'll be back for the second game of the Divisional series.

MONDAY 11 DECEMBER 1989

London have won their first two Divisional games, against the Midlands and the South West. Unfortunately, the competition doesn't seem to have come alive at all. I haven't felt fully involved in it; I haven't felt stretched, and I haven't played at my best. A lot of the other senior London players feel the same; although we've won both games by about twenty points, we haven't really got into top gear or put a game plan together. It's even more perplexing that the other divisions have lost so heavily and not looked particularly committed. This is meant to be our premier domestic competition, in which the sixty best players in England should be fighting for international places. Yet at the moment very few of these players seem to be putting enough thought or even effort into their Divisional rugby.

I get the uncomfortable feeling that the current England internationals are quite a few steps ahead of the other players in the Divisionals – that a large gap is opening up between the England squad and the rest. That is something we can't allow to happen. You need strength in depth if you are going to mount a serious challenge for a Five Nations – let alone a World Cup.

SUNDAY 17 DECEMBER 1989

London beat the North yesterday, in a very hard-fought game, to clinch the Divisional Championship. It was very wet and greasy, which cut down our ability to run the ball. The North had done their homework, and shut down my game. Rob Andrew played superbly well for them, and Peter Winterbottom also had a great game, but we had the edge in most areas of the pitch. I was relieved to win, because I was a Northerner myself once – which may explain the very warm welcome I got from Wade Dooley.

I'm glad the Divisionals are over, and that most of our top players seem to have come through without serious injury.

Last night the selection committee met to choose the twenty-eight players to go to Lanzarote. There was much debate about the front five. If nothing else, the Divisional championship proved that Jeff Probyn and Paul Rendall are still the best props we have: technically, they are on a different level to the rest, and the other pack members want these two props playing in the Five Nations. I am still worried about their fitness. Our first game in the World Cup is against New Zealand, and we simply cannot afford to carry any passengers in that game. Paul Rendall will have to work very hard to be fit enough to cope with the All Black pack in twenty-one months time, when he'll be thirty-seven. I hope he makes it, but we've certainly got to look for cover at loose-head prop. Jeff Probyn has been playing some of the best rugby of his career, and has a better chance of lasting until the World Cup. Brian Moore, in particular, insists that Jeff is the best tight-head in the business. I confess that front-row play is largely a mystery to me, but I have been impressed with the improvement in Jeff's attitude. Still, looking to the future, we'll be taking two second-string props: Mullins and Linnett. We're also taking a young second-row, Wasps' Sean O'Leary, who has a lot of potential, though he has only played in one Divisional game. Apart from that, I think the squad is fairly predictable. Five places have been left open, and we'll be filling them after the England B game against Russia next Saturday. In that match we'll be looking closely at David Pears at fly-half and Simon Langford at full back.

WEDNESDAY 21 DECEMBER 1989

A reminder of how painful selection can be. Andy Robinson rang me up. He has been left out of the squad for Lanzarote, and nobody has spoken to him since the Fiji game on 4 November, when he was also omitted. He is very upset. I haven't seen him play this year, though I've heard that his form hasn't been as sharp as it was last season. Be that as it may, there has been a regrettable failure of communication. Andy said that he felt he must have upset someone because of the complete absence of contact or explanation. He had a very fair point. Selectors need to talk to the players they omit, as well as to the ones they choose. They should give dropped players some point to work at, so that they know how they have to improve to get back into the side. This could only help the strength and depth of the England squad. Besides, in five weeks' time we might need to call on a player like Andy Robinson, and if he is still brooding about the way he has been neglected, the tensions could infect the whole team.

FRIDAY 5 JANUARY 1990, LANZAROTE

We arrived in Lanzarote yesterday afternoon, and at once we did our VO2 fitness tests, which were very disappointing; it seems most of the squad are no fitter than we were in September. Of course there are excuses – Christmas, New Year, the fact that we'd just got off the plane – but if our self-discipline has been what it should be none of these ought to be a factor. These four or five days' intensive training may turn out to be more of a necessity than a luxury.

The selectors met this morning to choose the side for the first Five Nations game, against Ireland in a fortnight's time. The two areas where there was most discussion were those where we have strength in depth – centre and the back row. There were valid arguments for both Guscott and Halliday in midfield – they're players of such different styles. In the end we went for Jerry's cutting edge over Simon's direct strength in attack and defence. In the back row, Micky Skinner has been playing outstandingly well this season, and Peter Winterbottom is a player of the very highest class who's hungry again after a slight falling-off last year. At Number 8, Dave Egerton's height, the fact that he has a club partnership with Richard Hill our scrum-half, and the fact that his rival Mike Teague, after his shoulder problem, isn't really as fit yet as he'd want to be, all worked in his favour.

The side will be announced after the morning session tomorrow, which will be an anxious time for me. It's not easy for me to cope with my dual role as player and selector – having to make cold-blooded decisions about blokes I play with, blokes I'd consider personal friends. Yesterday's selection didn't quite go my way, and I found it hard to walk away with a smile. Geoff Cooke recognises my problem. Being a selector as well as captain takes me further away from the other players than I like. After a game I go round to congratulate some and cheer up others as necessary; but when you're captain, no one pats you on the back however well you play. Accept captaincy, and you have to take the problems that come with the job. One of those is that to gain respect you have to sacrifice popularity. Certain players will never approve of you, and you can't let that bother you. I'm feeling the pressure of that at the moment – it's something I have to deal with.

MONDAY 8 JANUARY 1990

The last four days have been excellent – very well organised, with lots of different types of session to break up the hard work. There's a real seriousness emerging about getting the right attitude, most of which is to do with fitness. Our schedule from now until the World Cup is really strenuous, with two summer tours – Argentina and Australia – and no real break. And to equip us for that Tom McNab is devising an individual fitness programme for each of us – and if someone doesn't achieve the goals set for him, he'll be dropped from the squad.

But of course there have been lighter moments. Yesterday's training took the form of five-a-side football. I picked the sides and mine got into the final, where we lost 3-1. Weak refereeing from Mark Bailey.

Merlene Ottey, the Jamaican 200-metre runner, has been here doing her final preparation for the Commonwealth Games. Unknown to her, some of the front-five chaps were modelling her kit at the bar at 2.30 this morning – John Olver doing gymnastics in a bright-green leotard. I hope they didn't stretch her things too much; I notice she hasn't appeared on the track this morning.

The beds here have been a talking-point – eighteen inches wide, and every time you move the sheets fall off. Just what you need after four or five hours' training. Some of us have been stiff as boards from the sessions anyway – Mark Bailey needed help to put his shoes on last night. Anyway, the trip has put us in good spirits and I'm looking forward to meeting up again in nine days' time – the Wednesday before we play Ireland.

WEDNESDAY 17 JANUARY 1990

First training session for the Irish game at the Harlequins' ground. I had a talk with the players beforehand. As usual, we have been put under a lot of pressure by the media. But this time I feel our side is good enough to justify all the hype and win the Championship.

The next few days will be vital. We have to build foundations of confidence that will last all the way through the tournament. I can't remember the last time England won their first game of the Championship. Last year we expected to win our opening match against Scotland, and they held us to a 12-all draw at Twickenham, which set us back on our heels for the rest of the campaign. In the past, there have sometimes been question-marks against England's will to win – a feeling that players have been content with accumulating caps, instead of having a real raw determination to succeed in an England shirt. But on tonight's training performance I think we are getting there.

I did an awful, bland television interview this evening, but that's nothing new. I'm afraid that communicating with the media is not one of my strongest suits as a captain. But now I've got to put that out of my mind and concentrate on what to say to the team, jointly and individually, over the next forty-eight hours or so.

FRIDAY 19 JANUARY 1990, RICHMOND

For home internationals we always stay at the Petersham Hotel, Richmond. And part of my ritual here is to go for a walk at around ten o'clock at night, listening to music on my Walkman – tonight it was The Mission. I wander around under Richmond Hill, or sometimes I drift down into Richmond itself, for an hour or so. At these times I often think back to when I was six or seven, when I used to dream about internationals. Then I remind myself of all the people I've met on the way up. This helps me to savour the importance of the event, to enjoy each game to the full. After all, you never know which game is going to be your last.

I started playing rugby when I was at my prep school at Terra Nova, in Cheshire, near Joddrell Bank. My father was in the army, and we used to travel around; since we had grandparents living in Cheshire, it was thought there would be a base there for my brother and me. My father had played for Cardiff and the army, and actually got an England trial, but was injured before the match and didn't

PETERSHAM HOTEL

get another chance; but he didn't push us to play rugby. I arrived at school at seven and started playing the game straight away. I remember in my first match – a sort of ten-a-side touch thing – getting hold of the ball and *not passing*. I used to quite enjoy tackling, too – I was big for my age, then. There was a boy of my age called Bob Taylor, who was very good, which annoyed me. We were always put on different sides, and I would keep a note of how many

30

tries he scored, and I had to get more than him. (We're still great friends.) Every game then was for England at Twickenham; it was a hell of a long tunnel – about half a mile from the changing rooms to the pitch – but I can tell you the crowd was roaring all the way. Especially when, at eleven years old, I was allowed to wear metal studs, which rang out as you jogged along the concrete.

I started off as hooker, and played every position in the scrum, apart from second-row, and then I settled down at fly-half until my third year at Sedbergh, the public school in Yorkshire, when I made the switch to centre. By that time my whole week at school revolved around Saturday. Monday and Tuesday we trained, but the game was a long way away. Wednesday there would be a practice game, which was a good substitute for the real thing. Thursday we only got a miserable short session, though by then, for me, lessons were totally irrelevant. Friday was great, spent in blissful anticipation, watching the weather, and cleaning our boots. I always got mine spotless, and I'd fill them with newspaper – with the *Telegraph*, in fact, which was all we were allowed to read – and put them on a radiator, which was really bad for them, but which was the done thing. And then you'd come back at nine-thirty, and polish them until lights out, or even afterwards . . .

And then it was The Game, and then the discussion of your own central contribution, how, if you didn't score a try, you had made everyone else's by your speed and timing, etc.; how, if you lost, it was everyone else's fault but yours. Sunday was Chapel, praying for the next six days to go quickly. And that's how I got through five years at school; not much wonder I didn't become an academic.

At Sedbergh I used to play for the year-group above my own: for the Under-15s when I was an Under-14. Then I played two years in the Under-16s, coached by a guy called

Dick Mowbray, who moved me from fly-half to centre, where he thought I'd have more space to run. At the end of my second year under Dick, I played my first game for Sedbergh 1st XV. They'd dropped a boy who had his colours – the coveted brown blazer – to make room for me. I've never been so nervous before a game, not to this day. My mother says she remembers me walking along the riverbank with her, confused, not sure whether I wanted to play or not. We lost the game. The fly-half kept missing me out because he reckoned, rightly or wrongly, I'd be too nervous to catch the ball.

Next season I kept my place, and the colour wore his blazer in the 2nd XV. Sedbergh were unbeaten throughout my two years in the 1st XV, until the Lent term of my last year, when I was made captain for two games: we lost them both. Those two defeats were my last experience of captaincy until I did the job for England four years later.

But I'd already captained England Schoolboys before I'd captained Sedbergh. I remember my trial for Yorkshire Public Schools, in the pouring rain on Headingley's third-team pitch. And then my trial for Yorkshire Schoolboys. After that game, we were all sitting anxiously round a trestle table in a small room when the selectors came in and without any preamble said, 'This is the side,' and read out the names. Mine was the third or fourth. I couldn't believe it – a very happy moment.

Later that year I was picked for England Schoolboys, with Kevin Simms as my partner in the centre. Next year he went on to university at Cambridge, while I captained the Schoolboys. Then I had a year off before university, and I was in Australia when I got a letter from a friend telling me that Kevin had been picked for the full England side. I immediately thought – I've played with this guy, and now he's playing with the big boys. And naturally I began to wonder whether I might be good enough to do the same – that maybe there wasn't the chasm I'd always imagined between schoolboy level and the real thing.

At the time I was working my way round the world, as you're meant to do in the year between school and university – my brother had done it two years before. I went through Dubai, Hong Kong, Kuala Lumpur, Singapore, Australia, New Zealand, Hawaii, America. I had a great time, and when I got back I was fourteen stone. (I'm fourteen stone again now, but this was the wrong kind of weight.) I hadn't played any rugby, and I hadn't watched any either, not even in New Zealand.

I do remember sitting in a bar in Australia, though, watching the England-Australia match from Twickenham on the telly – this was 1984 – and talking to this Scots guy. We'd had a few drinks, and I happened to mention that I'd played for England Schoolboys, as you do, and he asked me if I thought I'd ever play for England, and I took another gulp of beer and said, 'No chance'. And he said, 'Well, I've got two younger brothers and they're both definitely going to play for Scotland, no doubt about it'. And I said 'Yeah, yeah', but he insisted. So I asked their names, and he said, 'Gavin and Scott Hastings'.

When I got back I did the army bit. I joined the Royal Regiment of Wales, and went up to Durham University on an Army Scholarship in the autumn of 1985. (Incidentally, my attachment to the army was to end when they refused me time to play representative rugby. A bit short-sighted of them, I think, when you consider how much free publicity the R.A.F. have had from Rory Underwood flying down the wing). I played for the university side against some real hard opposition up there, the Blaydons and the like, who'd come out for a juicy bit of student-bashing. That taught me how to take a good rucking, if nothing else. They played me at full back that year, and I have to admit I didn't enjoy it at all. They didn't play the expansive game I'd been used to with Sedbergh and the England Schoolboys. I wanted to run, but every time I did I was ticked off. At the end of the season I got county trials for Durham, but that was it; and I remember thinking at that stage, well, if this is what it's all about, forget it.

At the beginning of the next year, I had very little enthusiasm; I'd always been a keen trainer, but in the summer of '86 I did almost nothing. Then I went back to Sedbergh to play a one-off game for the Old Boys against the Luddites, and it was a beautiful sunny day, and we threw the ball about, and I loved it. When I returned to Durham, they played me in the centre, and things began to improve. I was picked for the county, and played against Lancashire. John Elliott and Geoff Cooke were the North selectors at the time, and they watched the game, and though I say it myself I had a blinder. As a result I was picked for the North, ahead of Fran Clough, Brian Barley and other internationals. I made the final trial that winter, but I wasn't picked for the 1987 Championship, and I didn't make the World Cup squad. But next year I played for the North again, and I got my first cap in my last year at university.

It was while I was playing for the North that I was advised by Mike Weston, who was then Chairman of the England selectors, to play for Harlequins. I wasn't going to argue with him. So I was up and down on the train sometimes three times a week: leaving Durham at 3 o'clock, getting to London and across London for training, and catching the last train home to arrive at three in the morning – great fun. But it worked.

My first cap was against France in Paris in 1988. In the trial I'd been in the B team with Kevin Simms, and John Buckton and Simon Halliday had been the first choices; but they both got hamstring injuries and pulled out. It was Geoff Cooke's first game as manager, and I thought my cap would be a one-off. We were expected to get hammered, so there was no pressure. I was thrilled to be in the same side as Peter Winterbottom and Rory Underwood – people who'd been heroes of mine when I was still at school – and I went through the whole weekend with a fixed smile.

I was sharing a room with Kevin Simms at the beautiful hotel in Versailles where we were staying. I remember putting the England tracksuit on, and looking in the mirror, and seeing nothing under the rose insignia – not SCHOOL-BOYS, not UNDER–21, not B or whatever. This was England, pure and simple. I hardly felt nervous about the game – but I had so much adrenalin I was sure I'd never sleep that night. As it was, I went out for a walk, and got back about eleven, and Kevin was reading away – next thing I knew I was awake again and it was ten in the morning. From then until kick-off, I was simply shaking with adrenalin, excited in a very positive way, really looking forward to the experience. And then we were out of the changing room, into the light of the stadium and the indescribable noise . . .

The game went by in a blur. I was concentrating so hard, and then it was suddenly over. We'd lost, 10-9; they scored a try late on to win. I think the guys who'd been around a long time, like Peter Winterbottom, were very disappointed, but all I could think of afterwards was – I survived that, I didn't play badly, it had been very exciting – and I wanted more. That's hardly the attitude that prevails now, of course; no one in the England camp could be happy in defeat. But for me, it was a great day. I don't remember anything about the evening.

And these are the things that I revolve in my mind as I

walk on my own in the night before an international at Twickenham.

SATURDAY 20 JANUARY 1990, TWICKENHAM

ENGLAND 23   **IRELAND** 0

Tries:	Probyn
	Egerton
	Underwood
	Guscott
Conversions:	Hodgkinson (2)
Penalty Goal:	Hodgkinson

This was a disappointing Irish performance, their hestitancy embodied in Russell who made a very nervous debut at fly-half. And yet the Irish managed to hold England until the last ten minutes, when Carling, Guscott and Underwood suddenly found their feet and England added three tries to Jeff Probyn's first-half pick-up and dive. The first of these was scored by Dave Egerton the Number 8, after a succession of tapped penalties near the Irish line. Then the backs carved out two beautiful scores. Guscott made one with a searing break and well-judged high pass to his right to Underwood, who ran in at pace to become England's leading try-scorer of all time with nineteen tries in inter-

nationals. Then a slashing run by Carling made space for Guscott to cross for another.

These last few minutes obliterated the rest of the match for an enthralled crowd, and raised high expectations for England's performance in the remainder of the Championship.

ENGLAND: S. D. Hodgkinson (Nottingham); R. Underwood (Leicester), W. D. C. Carling (Harlequins) *(capt)*, J. C. Guscott (Bath), M. D. Bailey (Wasps); C. R. Andrew (Wasps), R. J. Hill (Bath); P. A. G. Rendall (Wasps), B. C. Moore (Nottingham), J. A. Probyn (Wasps), P. J. Ackford (Harlequins), W. A. Dooley (Preston Grasshoppers), M. G. Skinner (Harlequins), P. J. Winterbottom (Harlequins), D. W. Egerton (Bath)

IRELAND: K. Murphy (Constitution); M. J. Kiernan (Dolphin), B. J. Mullin (Blackrock Coll), D. G. Irwin (Instonians), K. D. Crossan (Instonians); P. Russell (Instonians), L. F. P. Aherne (Lansdowne); D. C. Fitzgerald (Lansdowne), S. J. Smith (Ballymena), G. Halpin (Wanderers), N. P. T. Francis (Blackrock Coll), W. A. Anderson (Dungannon) *(capt)*, P. M. Matthews (Wanderers), P. T. J. O'Hara (Sunday's Well), N. P. Mannion (Corinthians)

Replacement: J. P. MacDonald (Malone) for Smith

Referee: P. Robin (France)

Other Match: WALES 19 FRANCE 29

SUNDAY 21 JANUARY 1990

So we got the campaign under way successfully, with a very good win. To score twenty-three points in a Championship game these days you have to play pretty well. I see the press have written off the Irish this morning, but as far as I'm concerned they played with skill, character and pride, as they always do. There were some areas of our game which didn't go according to plan. Our pack, especially the front five, had been looked at as the most powerful force in the championship, but I think they would admit that they didn't really click yesterday, especially in the line-out. Wade Dooley was not as dominant as usual, and although there will be some talk about the French referee's liberal interpretation of the line-out laws, that doesn't detract from the Irish effort. Neil Francis is a top-class line-out performer. Although we were very strong in the scrum, it wasn't the irresistible power-base that a lot of people were expecting. That may be to our future advantage, because if we had annihilated Ireland up front we might have started to believe the press, and then we could have had motivational problems in the later games. The backs, on the other hand, have at last begun to fulfil their potential. In the past eighteen months or so, we've produced a lot of good rugby, but the last quarter of an hour on Saturday is about the best we've been.

It took us a long time to gain any dominance in the set piece, which was a little frustrating. I remember trying to put a grubber-kick through for Jerry, which was a move we'd planned, but it bounced off David Irwin, the Irish centre. Simon Hodgkinson had come up into the line and we had no cover. I turned round to see the ball bounce away from me with most of the Irish team in pursuit – a horrible moment. Luckily, Rob Andrew got back in time, and fell superbly, and eventually I got back with him. We each took a bit of a knock, but I was almost glad of the opportunity to take a pounding to redeem my error of judgement.

We were desperate to win, and we strove too hard at first, urgent to get points on the board, but without taking the risks you need to take at this level. Defences are so well organised and there is such a lot of commitment in the tackle that, unless you take the odd calculated gamble, you are unlikely to manufacture tries. Our anxiety to do well showed in the forty minutes that elapsed between Simon Hodgkinson's penalty that made it 7-0, halfway through the first half, and Dave Egerton's try from the short penalty. At that point the burden of expectation and the anxiety just fell away, and we began to run the ball with confidence. First I got a quick ball from Rob, and passed to Jerry, who made a half-break and threw out a beautiful lobbed pass for Rory to score his nineteenth try for England – a record – with a great run. Then, towards the end, I got the ball from Rob in broken play and, as sometimes happens, I got the sense of a little bit of space outside for Jerry and Rory. I tried to hold the man in front of me, feinted inside then out and just got past him, and slipped the ball to Jerry as I sensed another tackler approaching me. Then he accelerated like an arrow through the gap and scored our fourth try.

Throughout the game, Richard Hill's length and speed

of pass gave Rob Andrew an extra yard-and-a-half to make his decisions, and Rob is flourishing with the new space he is getting. Best of all, it now feels as if the whole side knows exactly what we are trying to do in every area of the pitch. We know when to attack down a particular channel, and what we are trying to do with second-phase ball. That gives us real confidence.

Certain moments of the game stick in my mind as turning-points. I think Michael Kiernan's missing his third penalty, an easy one, when we were still only 3-0 up, was crucial. Then there was Micky Skinner's tackle on Philip Matthews from a five-yard scrum after Ireland had produced a good back-move to get down into the right-hand corner. Micky shunted Matthews – who's the hard man of the Irish side – back a good five yards. We won the ruck ball and they couldn't get back into our twenty-two after that. Not the least pleasing aspect of the game was that we didn't concede a single point – a rare feat in an international.

SATURDAY 27 JANUARY 1990

I've been talking to Geoff Cooke and Roger Uttley about selection for the match against France. Mike Teague is fit again, and we have decided to include him at Number 8 in place of Dave Egerton rather than bringing him in on the flank. The decision could have gone either way, but we felt that with the size and power that the French have in the back row, we needed to match them with the immense upper-body strength of Teague and Mick Skinner. Despite all his other virtues, we felt that Dave Egerton just didn't have the physical power for the close-quarter contest. Of course we'll be losing height in the line-out, but the French are so tall all the way down the line that we are not going to try to compete with them at the back anyway. Instead we are going to try and stop the man who comes around, and hit him behind the gain line. Still, it was a very hard decision. Roger Uttley took Dave Egerton aside and broke the news, and I spoke to Dave later on. Naturally he is very disappointed, but he has taken it extremely well. It was hard for me to sit there and console him at the bar; I hope he gets another chance soon. I know he'll turn up at training tomorrow and be as constructive and committed as usual. We all know that if you lose your place you have to fight to get it back. That's a healthy state of affairs.

FRIDAY 2 FEBRUARY 1990, PARIS

We flew out yesterday afternoon after a training session at Hampton School.

The coach took us from the airport to our hotel near the palace at Versailles. The away game in Paris is quite unlike any other match in the Championship. There are none of the little diversions that normally help to keep you calm in the build-up to a game – whether it's English TV, or a cinema nearby, or chicken sandwiches and coffee, or room service without a phrase-book. You can't wander down to the shops or bars to chat casually with locals. You're thrown together with the other players – plus the management and the medical people – and as a result, all you can talk about is The Game. That's hard work.

Ridiculously – and especially on Saturday morning, when the breakfast is so important – some of us get irritated by the fact that the waiters don't understand what we want, not stopping to consider that we can't make ourselves understood in French – trying to get brown toast or whatever. The evening after the match is different, of course: by about midnight it's a mercy that not many people can understand what we're saying.

After our last training session this afternoon – a crisp, encouraging work-out – we went down to the Parc des Princes and had a look around. The ground is quite soggy, but it should be firmer tomorrow. The forwards have sorted out all sorts of line-out ploys with Brian. Mike Teague, Mick Skinner and Peter Winterbottom have gone over the variations of defence at the back of the line-out, and are prepared for anything the French can throw at us there. Wade Dooley and Paul Ackford are also ready for ploys at the front and middle of the line. The backs have studied videos of French moves, and we're aiming to attack down Denis Charvet's channel. Charvet plays left centre, with Philippe Sella as right centre. This means that from the right-hand side of the field we will be attacking their inside centre position through me, and from the left-hand side of the field we will be aiming to attack their outside centre through Jerry.

When it comes to kicking in general play, we want to put the kicks in front of Blanco, and between him and his wingers. We don't want to kick low and straight to him, because he comes onto kicks very well; if we kick high between him and the winger it tends to cause confusion. And Blanco doesn't like hanging around under a ball waiting to be hit. It's not quite his style.

I had a particularly good talk with Paul Ackford; he fed me back some ideas from the forwards, who are really keyed up for this one. There is an intense buzz of anticipation through the team; an eagerness to get out there and prove to people that we have really got it right this time.

SATURDAY 3 FEBRUARY 1990: MORNING

We beat the French at Twickenham last year, but they are a different beast here in Paris. They haven't been beaten here since 1982, and that sort of record gives a side the belief that they aren't going to lose. We have got to crack that. I'm sure we will be able to put them under pressure. It would really instil confidence if we could get three or six or nine points on the board after fifteen minutes. That would calm our nerves and allow us to play a more controlled game without the panic of trying to make our mark on the scoreboard. It's vital that Simon Hodgkinson kicks his goals today. Unfortunately, it's very windy this morning, so it doesn't look as if goalkicking's going to be easy.

SATURDAY 3 FEBRUARY 1990, PARC DES PRINCES

FRANCE 7		ENGLAND 26	
Try:	Lagisquet	Tries:	Underwood
Penalty Goal:	Charvet		Guscott
			Carling
		Conversion:	Hodgkinson
		Penalty Goals:	Hodgkinson (4)

This was one of the greatest of all English performances in international rugby, a record victory for England at the Parc des Princes, and the finest flourishing yet of Will Carling's side. Moore was outstanding in a dominant pack, but the whole side exuded self-belief and authority after Simon Hodgkinson put them into an early 9–0 lead with three penalties effortlessly slotted through a strong, swirling wind. Soon after, Rob Andrew, in a moment of vision, thumped the ball deep down the vacant French left wing, where Rory Underwood, following up, was able to touch down unopposed. 13–0 at half-time, and there was more to come. Early in the second half an intended chip-kick by Charvet rebounded off Carling, and Guscott was on hand to hack forward, gather a favourable bounce and score by the posts. Home spirits were briefly raised by a try by the left wing Lagisquet, but the last word belonged to the

England captain. England were pounding the French line when Andrew switched to the right in midfield. One of the French forwards halted him with a trip, but he fed Carling, whose shimmy and break left Blanco standing as he crossed for England's third try.

FRANCE: S. Blanco (Biarritz); M. Andrieu (Nimes), P. Sella (Agen), D. Charvet (Toulouse), P. Lagisquet (Bayonne); F. Mesnel (Racing Club de France), P. Berbizier (Agen) (*capt*); P. Ondarts (Biarritz), L. Armary (Lourdes), J-P. Garuet (Lourdes), T. Devergie (Nimes), D. Erbani (Agen), O. Roumat (Dax), E. Champ (Toulon), L. Rodriguez (Dax) (*capt*)

Replacement: P. Marocco (Montferrand) for Armary

ENGLAND: S. D. Hodgkinson (Nottingham); R. Underwood (Leicester), W. D. C. Carling (Harlequins) (*capt*), J. Guscott (Bath), M. D. Bailey (Wasps); C. R. Andrew (Wasps), R. J. Hill (Bath); P. A. G. Rendall (Wasps), B. C. Moore (Nottingham), J. A. Probyn (Wasps), P. J. Ackford (Harlequins), W. A. Dooley (Preston Grasshoppers), M. G. Skinner (Harlequins), P. J. Winterbottom (Harlequins), M. C. Teague (Gloucester)

Referee: O. E. Doyle (Ireland)

Other Match: IRELAND 10 SCOTLAND 13

MONDAY 5 FEBRUARY 1990

Even with my lingering hangover I can look over the game in Paris with great satisfaction. We accomplished our game plan and fulfilled nearly all our hopes. We put points on the board early on: Simon kicked two goals out of three in the first exchanges of the game, and the other one hit the post – superb kicking in the conditions. This allowed us to establish a domination up front which I have never before seen an away team achieve at international level. We may have had the older pack, but it was some of theirs who looked past their sell-by date. Our pack took the line-outs 19–9. Berbizier was always scrabbling around for what little ball he was given, and Mesnel, as a result, was getting bad service under immense pressure from Peter Winterbottom and Mick Skinner. The reverberations of this were felt throughout the whole French side. Their three-quarters never got a chance to move, and our backs harrowed them terrifically. Rendall and Probyn ruled the scrum: the French eight was never solid. Our first-time tackling was superb. Micky Skinner's tackle on Armary, the tough hooker, who had to go off as a result, was an immense hit. Throughout the game, and right across the pitch, the French were really hitting the floor.

Once we'd got ahead, the confidence we'd had towards the end of the Irish game began to surface again. Then Rob dummied from the line-out and went up the blind side, and chipped over Lagisquet for Rory to chase. I remember looking down the field and wondering where the French cover had got to, when Rory hared down the wing straight past Lagisquet, and I suddenly thought, My God, there's a try on here. It was Blanco who was miles out of position. When Rory touched down the score was suddenly 10–0 and we had the chance of going 12–0 up. I couldn't believe the French had left the whole of their left-hand side of the pitch unmarked; but it was a great piece of vision by Rob. From that point on, we knew we were going to win.

One incident that's attracted a bit of comment is a tackle I made on Berbizier. Everyone knew that he was the French playmaker, that all their tactics revolved around him, and it might have looked as if we were trying to nail him. I put up a kick and Marc Andrieu caught it. I actually thought the ball was going to go out on the full, so I wasn't chasing it quite as fast as I might have done. When I saw Andrieu catch the ball I accelerated towards him. Mark Bailey got to him first. The ball spilled free and Berbizier got his hands to it, and I had to run into him to knock him off the ball. It wasn't meant maliciously at all, and it certainly wasn't as dramatic an incident as it may have appeared on television. Berbizier dived as if he'd been poleaxed. It made me feel terribly powerful, for about three seconds. But I knew I hadn't hurt him.

Just after half-time, when we were 12–0 up, the French got a bit of slow possession and came down the right flank. Berbizier passed it out to Mesnel, who shipped it on to Charvet. Rob, Jerry and I were moving up and across the field. Charvet tried to kick ahead and it rebounded off me. I chased after it with Jerry and I couldn't work out why Blanco was dawdling so casually near the ball. Jerry got his foot to it and booted it ahead and was away. Just as when Rory scored our first try, I couldn't believe the French cover was so lax, or that they could be so timid about tidying up the bouncing ball. Jerry had plenty of time to score. Simon kicked the goal – 19–0. Then, just a few minutes before the end, Mike Teague picked up from a scrum and we drove on through Richard Hill. I remember moving out to the right to try and draw a bit of cover for Rob and Jerry, who were out on the left. Then, Jerry came round to join me on the right, and Richard fired the ball out to Rob on the left. By now, of course, he didn't have much support on that side, so I called to him and he switched to come right. One of their second-rows tripped him up, but he popped the ball up to me, and as I took it

I glanced up and saw Blanco coming up very quickly. I knew Jerry was outside me but I sensed that he was being marked by Lagisquet, and because Blanco was coming at such pace I dummied and he fell for it. And I was clear. There was no cover, and I just accelerated in for the try. It's that great old feeling – *Whoof – I'm going to score.*

The final score was 26–7. No team had ever beaten France by so many points at the Parc des Princes, and it was England's biggest margin of victory over them since 1914. Perhaps surprisingly, the atmosphere in the changing room afterwards was very subdued. There were no howls of joy or anything like that, but when Geoff Cooke said that he thought it was perhaps England's finest performance ever in international rugby, I felt very proud. Jacques Fouroux, the French coach, said that if we'd changed our shirts from white to black we could have been New Zealand. Meanwhile down in the changing room Brian Moore and Peter Winterbottom were already talking about the game against Wales at Twickenham in a fortnight's time, which was very encouraging to me as captain.

We absorbed the news that Scotland had beaten Ireland 13–10. The 1990 Championship was beginning to take shape.

Rob a | SHATTERED AFTER FRANCE.

SATURDAY 10 FEBRUARY 1990

The England squad have just met, and the selectors have been assessing the performance against France. It's tempting to give a rubber stamp to the side and say, 'Great performance in Paris. Let's do the same again.' But we have to avoid complacency, and look at ways to tune the side finer and finer. The general feeling is that Mark Bailey is struggling to perform at the moment. He has had a few injury problems, especially with his hamstring, but I don't think that's the problem. I think he is lacking in confidence right now, and when you're playing in such an intense tournament as the Five Nations you don't have time to find your form. You must be on song when you start and you've got to strive very hard to maintain that level all the way through. Mark's not there at the moment, and with a player of Simon Halliday's calibre on the bench, with his overall strength in attack and defence, and the options he would give us on the right wing, the general feeling is that we must give Simon a go. He's a very powerful man, his ball-retention is exemplary, and he offers many variations off his open-side wing down the middle of the field. On the blind-side wing, his passing skills and his decision-making in tight spaces are top-class, and his defensive qualities have never been in question. I have chatted to Mark. He is bitterly disappointed, as dropped players always will be, but although he will never agree with it, I'm sure he understands the thinking behind the change. It's very hard for players of the calibre of Dave Egerton, Mark Bailey and Steve Bates to be on the bench instead of playing international rugby, when they would get into most of the sides that we play against. It doesn't help me that they are such nice guys, that they never complain or give me a hard time.

THURSDAY 15 FEBRUARY 1990

The build-up to the Welsh game. We trained last night and today, in awful conditions – an absolutely freezing wind. Nonetheless morale is very high, as you might expect, though we're taking nothing for granted.

Last year, we went into the Welsh game rather haphazardly. It was the last game of the Five Nations, and we went into it rather surprised to be in a position to win the Championship. This year, we have been much more thoughtful in our approach to each game. We've worked together under Geoff to pinpoint the strengths and weaknesses of the sides we've played, and the best ways of attacking them, and the best way to defend when they try to strike against us. In the first two games this has obviously gone very well, and we have approached this Welsh game just as meticulously. As a result there's a quiet, steely confidence running through the side.

There has been a lot of hype – there always is before a Welsh game, which I find infuriating. There is the usual talk of our psychological problem with the Welsh. Maybe in the Seventies, when the Welsh had a great side, the English had a wee complex, the same complex that any side has against patently superior opposition; nowadays, that's not the case. I have played against them twice, and I've lost twice, but I don't think those defeats have had

51

psychological causes. Last year there was awful weather, and a number of other factors: we lost Mike Teague in the first minute with his head cut open, Paul Ackford had a very painful elbow, and I had food poisoning. This year we don't have those niggling problems; and with luck we won't lose a key player in the first few seconds of the game. Fending off media questions about how to break down the Welsh jinx has been galling – when I don't believe the problem exists – and it has tested my tactfulness to the full.

Not that I would write off the Welsh. They have some very good players. They have certain drills which they perform very well, and they have good backs. Their scrum is solid, and behind it Robert Jones is a world-class player. But as far as Welsh sides go, this one is not quite average.

I see certain areas as crucial. As always, we want to gain dominance up front, especially in the line-out, and we need a good firm scrummage platform. We are looking to move the ball wide early on to gain crowd support. I feel that's vital. The English support in Paris was unbelievable, and I know it gave the players a great lift. If we can get the crowd buzzing early on, it'll get us in the right frame of mind. So, Rob and I are looking to give Jerry, Simon Halliday and Rory Underwood a tilt as early as possible. And it's not just to please the crowd. We also feel that there's a doubt about the fitness of the Welsh pack, and if we can move them around for sixty minutes, they will struggle in the last twenty.

Other vital areas: we must pressurize Jones. Last year we let him get on top of his game, and we paid a heavy price when his kicks pinned us back time and again in the last twenty minutes.

Defensively I think we will be sound; I think we've got the right back-row combination. Richie Collins is a good player, but Peter Winterbottom is just about the best open-side flanker in the world. Tomorrow his role will be crucial. They have two fairly inexperienced second-rows in Llewellyn and Allen, and we must take advantage of that in the line-out. If we can dominate there, as we have in the first two games, we can then enforce our strategy on the whole game. And if we can put them under pressure and tire them out in the scrum, they are always going to be on the back foot when they try and use their backs. That's what happened to the French. Obviously, the first twenty minutes of any game are pretty hectic, but at the moment I feel that we are good enough and experienced enough to exert control from the start.

I'm waiting to see what the weather will throw at us. The forecast is that it will be dry. That would suit us fine, and I think it would lead to a high-quality, open game. Whatever the conditions, it's going to be a passionate one.

SATURDAY 17 FEBRUARY 1990, TWICKENHAM

ENGLAND 34		WALES 6	
Tries:	Carling	Try:	Davies
	Underwood (2)	Conversion:	Thorburn
	Hill		
Conversions:	Hodgkinson (3)		
Penalty Goals:	Hodgkinson (4)		

England laid the bogey of recent Welsh successes against them in the most emphatic style. The backs again combined irresistibly, but they were supported in attack by forwards like Winterbottom and Moore and even the prop Rendall, whose evident fitness and footballing skills were a credit to Geoff Cooke's new regime. The Welsh forwards, on the other hand, with the unstinting exception of Phil Davies, looked callow and lacking in stamina.

England got their usual runaway start through successful penalties by Hodgkinson, and then Carling embarrassed the Welsh defence to score his second try of the Championship, bumping through several ineffectual tackles to cross in the left-hand corner. Two more tries by the lethal marksman Underwood continued the slaughter, then a beautiful spin pass by Winterbottom put the winger away to make the space for Hill to complete the rout. Wales had only a consolation try from the barging Davies to sweeten the pill; their coach John Ryan resigned in the days following this national disaster.

ENGLAND: S. D. Hodgkinson (Nottingham); S. J. Halliday (Bath), W. D. C. Carling (Harlequins) (*capt*), J. C. Guscott (Bath), R. Underwood (Leicester); C. R. Andrew (Wasps), R. J. Hill (Bath); P. A. G. Rendall (Wasps), B. C. Moore (Nottingham), J. A. Probyn (Wasps), P. J. Ackford (Harlequins), W. A. Dooley (Preston Grasshoppers), M. G. Skinner (Harlequins), P. J. Winterbottom (Harlequins), M. C. Teague (Gloucester)

WALES: P. H. Thorburn (Neath); M. H. Titley (Swansea), M. G. Ring (Cardiff), M. R. Hall (Cardiff), A. Emyr (Swansea); D. W. Evans (Cardiff), R. N. Jones (Swansea) (*capt*); M. Griffiths (Cardiff), K. H. Phillips (Neath), L. Delaney (Llanelli), G. O. Llewellyn (Neath), A. G. Allen (Newbridge), P. T. Davies (Llanelli), R. G. Collins (Cardiff), M. A. Jones (Neath)

Referee: D. Leslie (Scotland)

Other Match: SCOTLAND 21 FRANCE 0

TUESDAY 20 FEBRUARY 1990

I've had a few days to reflect on the Welsh game, so I'm not talking in the flush of victory when I say that I think people will look at this match for years to come and remember it as a turning-point in English rugby. Not only did we beat the Welsh for once, but we thrashed them comprehensively in every department of the game. And it seems to have given people a great deal of satisfaction. Public reaction has been remarkable. I can't walk far down the street before someone stops me to say: 'Thank you very much,' and I know what they are thanking me for. I have to say, 'Well it's a pleasure.' And it is.

As for the game itself, I don't think the importance – as in Paris – of Simon Hodgkinson kicking the first two penalties can be stressed too much. I appreciate the kind of pressure he is faced with when he takes those kicks in internationals. It's a kind of pressure most rugby players never have to deal with. It gives us such encouragement when he gives us the lead and we know that the other side will have to produce something to get back into the game.

Then, after about ten minutes, I got my try. It came out of nothing, really. Jerry took the ball into a ruck, and when it came back Rory had gone over to the right so I was on my own on the left. But Rob came my way and popped me the ball: I had Mark Jones coming at me and Mark Titley

55

covering too. But Jones had got his line completely wrong and I just moved away from him. Titley should certainly have had me, but he came very high and caught my hand-off and lost his balance. I was aware of hordes of Welsh shirts converging, and I thought I might as well keep going and hope we won the loose ball. Robert Jones was at me next – he dived in at my legs, but I managed to stay on my feet, and suddenly the line was only a few yards away. The way was blocked inside, so I dived at the corner and just managed to pop it down as the cover hit me. Simon converted from the touchline to make it 12–0, and that – after about ten minutes – was that.

Once we'd established our lead, I thought the level of fitness and concentration among the forwards was most impressive. Their driving play as a group was immense. The Welsh had some good passages of play, but they were working fragmentarily, in ones and twos, whereas when our forwards started driving, the continuity and solidity of the group of them was a joy to watch. And I still felt that we had another level of fitness in reserve that we could step up into.

We've also proved that we've got a new string to our bow; the ability to move the ball and make incisions through the three-quarters. This isn't done in a spirit of hit-and-hope; we move the ball deliberately to make ground. Running three-quarters are not only the most entertaining, but also the most effective way of playing the game.

I've been asked to pinpoint outstanding individuals and outstanding moments of the game. I'm a bit reluctant, since each part of a team is wholly reliant on the others. But here goes. One of the major differences in our performances this year is the fact that our front row are exerting so much pressure on the opposition. That means that their second row and back row have to work that much harder to stabilise their scrum; and their back row have to stay down a fraction of a second longer, which gives our middle three-quarters time and space in which to move. Also our line-out jumpers are so dominant, and the props are tidying up the line-out so well, that we as backs are receiving mint possession. And Richard Hill's service has been a revelation. His speed and accuracy, and the ability he has shown to make the right decision at the right time, have given Rob new confidence.

Whatever was once written about him in the press, I have always rated Rob as a class player; and I think he had turned the corner way before the Lions tour. But he is proving to everyone now the sort of control he can exert over a game. Simon Hodgkinson's kicking has been first-rate, and his defence has been very secure too. Some pundits said at the start of the season that our weakness would be under the high ball – well, our opponents have put the high ball up, and there has been no weakness, so Simon gets great credit there. But I could go through each member of the team and say, well, so-and-so was crucial here, and so-and-so was crucial there, and I think that each of us can take satisfaction from the fact that we have all played vital roles in each success. Even the reserves have been superb; their belief in, and their support of, the players on the pitch helps build a settled, positive atmosphere in the days before each international, and the value of that can't be overstated. When I look at the French, the Welsh and the Irish sides I see factions in them which must be detrimental to team spirit.

But back to this game. The line-out statistics suggest that the Welsh won as much ball, but they had nearly half as many put-ins again as we did. We were devastating in the scrummage. If we were honest with ourselves, we'd have to admit that we missed two or three clear-cut scoring opportunities. Oh, it's a very comfortable position to be in, having won 34-6, to be able to say we squandered a couple of tries. But when we come together in ten days' time for the next training session, there'll be faults that we'll all be keen to confront and iron out: you know, 'I should have delivered that pass earlier,' or 'I got my lines of running wrong.' Going left, we should twice have finished off moves in space that had been made by forward charges. And one strike against the head should have been converted into a try as well.

Although we were obviously delighted with the manner and the margin of this victory, we are still very aware that we have one more game to go. Friends have been saying to me: 'Have you come down to earth yet?' I'm down to earth all right. Obviously it was a great game, but if we lose to Scotland, three superb victories will count for nothing, and I think that all the players' celebrations were tempered with that knowledge. So it was a contented changing room, but by no means a euphoric one. We have certain areas to work on, and three weeks to get them right before going up to Murrayfield. A month is a long time between matches, but I hope we can make it work to our advantage.

WEDNESDAY 28 FEBRUARY 1990

On Saturday, we'll get together at the Petersham Hotel in Richmond to watch Wales v. Scotland, to train a bit, and to analyse the Scots in the evening. The Welsh have made five changes in their side, and look to have got rid of some of the brittleness in their pack. I'm expecting a pretty close contest, and I wouldn't be surprised if the Welsh, with the advantage of playing at home, pulled off a surprise win.

I'll be interested to see what the mood of the squad will be when we meet. I hope no one's getting carried away with all the publicity we've had, because we're still only three-quarters of the way there. There's been far too much talk about the Grand Slam for my liking, and it could yet rebound on us. But there are some experienced men in this squad, and I'm sure they'll be keeping their heads.

I see the fixture list has come up with one of its little treats: a round of Courage League matches the week before the biggest domestic international for ten years. Harlequins (for example) are away at Gloucester, which must count as one of the hardest club fixtures of the season. Most of the guys would want a game of some sort to keep sharp, but there are better places to do that than at the bottom of a ruck at Kingsholm. Still, I suppose the day when the fixture list is mapped out for the benefit of twenty-one individuals is, and probably ought to be, a long way away.

TUESDAY 6 MARCH 1990

Wales and Scotland produced a pretty disappointing game, which Scotland won narrowly (13-9). Neither side seemed able to apply any control. I was surprised that Scotland could dominate the set pieces so completely, yet still leave Wales the chance of winning the game the whole way through. The Welsh tactical plan was practically invisible: under such pressure in the scrum, they didn't seek to move the ball wide or loosen the game up at all. The Scots reinforced our view that they have a very fit pack. But I think they were flattered by their set-piece domination in this game, because the Welsh pack, even with so many changes, looked extremely raw. Scotland chase kicks very well, and they tackle hard in the midfield, but they don't seem to have a creative dimension to their game. Kicking seems to be their main attacking ploy.

We trained a bit on Saturday, and had a hard session on Sunday – two hours' worth, with a lot of bag work, and practising staying on our feet, which I think will be very important in the Scottish match. They want to get the ball on the floor, and we want to keep upright for our mauling game.

I was bothered to see the old question of amateurism come up again at this stage; it is one that I really wanted to avoid until after Murrayfield, because however amicably you discuss it, it is always going to raise a few hackles with certain guys with strong views, like Brian Moore and Paul Ackford. We've discussed it, and even between the three of us there has been some heated disagreement. It is the sort of issue that can interfere with the stability and unity of the side, and I hope that a short chat next week to the whole squad, to tell them the sort of stance we feel is applicable, will calm things down, and then after the Scottish game we can reassess things and realign ourselves accordingly. But it is a worrying point for me. I want to keep the team on an even keel, and I want to keep as many distractions out of their minds as possible.

My own view is that I never want to be paid for taking the pitch. I still play because I enjoy it, and I don't want a sort of rugby employer telling me where and when I have to play, but I think the RFU will have to relax the rules in other areas. I don't see any harm in a few players being able to make pocket money out of endorsements. The sums won't be large, and it'll only affect a handful of players at the top, and it won't change the game for the guys at Esher Thirds or wherever. The trouble is that different rules are operating in different countries. Look at the New Zealanders. Companies make them PR executives; they turn up at the odd lunch here and there, and the rest of the time they train. That's professionalism. That's why they're world champions. And we have to compete against them with guys who have to decide whether they can even afford to play rugby – not how much they're going to make out of it. International rugby is so time-consuming these days that you *have* to make career sacrifices if you want to stay at the top for any length of time. And when you think of the money coming into the game, of the millions that the World Cup will generate, it doesn't seem right that the players should still be forbidden from using their status to protect their livelihood. After all, the crowds don't come through the turnstiles to watch the great administrators.

Things will change, and all these issues need thinking over. But not in the week before a Grand Slam decider.

WEDNESDAY 14 MARCH 1990

It's the Wednesday before the Scottish game. We've met at the Harlequins' ground and had a good session. It's always hard to gauge the mood of a team this early in the preparation, while we've still got three days to go. I sense it's good. I didn't see too much of the forwards' training, but the backs are certainly very sharp and eager, as you would expect.

What the four-week break between matches will have done is anyone's guess. I think that if we win this game people will forget the fact that we had a month off. I would like to think it hasn't made any difference to us, that we have been able to maintain the momentum we've built up during the Championship, but I just don't know. We fly up to Scotland tomorrow; we're staying in Edinburgh this time, rather than in our traditional hotel thirty miles away in Peebles. Weather conditions are apparently going to be quite good. I hope it won't rain. Judging by the backs' session tonight, we'd thrive in dry conditions.

The media have certainly got their teeth into this one. Both sides are going for the Grand Slam, which has never happened between two British sides before. And there's more interest building up than for any match I've ever played in, more even than for last year's game in Wales. This is a really big one; and I feel confident and nervous in equal measures.

FRIDAY 16 MARCH 1990, EDINBURGH

We've had our last training session of the 1990 Championship; it went very well indeed. I don't think there was a ball dropped in forty-five minutes of really good work. Our moves were neatly executed, and everyone was concentrating to the full. Now each individual has to go away and steel himself for the challenge he is going to face on the pitch – though we can only guess at what Murrayfield's going to be like. I'm sure there's going to be an awful lot of passion around.

The Scots are obviously determined that their side should be seen as firm underdogs, which worries me greatly. No scenario would suit the Scots better than this: playing as outsiders in their own back yard against the English, who they would always give anything to beat. They are going to come out really psyched-up, and will play a disruptive game. It's going to be harder for us to establish our own pattern. I've been revolving in my mind how we are going to counter the Scots' passion; I try to tell the players that they have got to gird themselves inside, and they have got to know what is going to hit them – not least what sort of cauldron they are going to walk out into. They have got to be strong enough to shut the Scottish noise and antagonism out of their system, and concentrate on their own duties in the game. They have to do that on their own: there's nothing else that I, or Brian, Geoff Cooke or Roger Uttley can do for them. It's going to be one of the hardest games we have ever played. We have played great rugby and imposed ourselves on sides so far this season, and three weeks ago I didn't think the Scots would be able to withstand our overflowing confidence. But now I sense they'll be harder to dominate than the teams we've already beaten.

SATURDAY 17 MARCH 1990: MORNING

I have been trying to come up with new ideas to put to the players today to try and edge them on to a new level of confidence or ability. I do believe we have the most talented side in the Championship. Part of my job is to get that talent to work, four times on the run, against very different opposition each time. As a captain I've got to try to get myself to that level first, and then get everyone else up with me. But when all's said and done, it's each man for himself. You can have great captains, you can have inspirational pack leaders, you can have great coaches. But all the best-laid plans are at the mercy of the individuals who are meant to put them into practice.

As I said to the players last night, we have a chance today to establish ourselves as a great side. We haven't proved that yet. We are going to come up against a side who are going to reduce everything to chaos. I hope we've got the strength to respond; but it is going to be possibly the most emotionally draining, physically fraught eighty minutes any of us have ever been through, and I am sure we are going to learn a lot from it – win or lose.

SATURDAY 17 MARCH 1990, MURRAYFIELD

SCOTLAND 13		**ENGLAND** 7	
Try:	Stanger	**Try:**	Guscott
Penalty Goals:	Chalmers (3)	**Penalty Goal:**	Hodgkinson

With the Grand Slam, the Triple Crown, the Championship and the Calcutta Cup all to play for, this may have been the most eagerly-anticipated international ever played on British soil. The setting matched the occasion: the crowd at Murrayfield generated an extraordinary intensity, and from the moment that David Sole led his team out walking instead of sprinting, the supercharged Scots had the psychological edge over their opponents. The English front row, immovable throughout the season, splintered at the first scrummage, and conceded the first of several penalties for acts of indiscipline that were to cost England dear. Craig Chalmers converted two of these to give Scotland an early lead. England responded with a cracking try, Guscott dummying over after handling by Teague, Hill and Carling, but Scotland kept up their furious pace in the loose, and a further penalty for foul play allowed Chalmers to give them a 9–4 lead at half-time. With their scrum waxing stronger and the wind in their favour, the English seemed likely to come back in the second half, but immediately after the interval the Scots engineered a try for Stanger, after good work on the short side by Armstrong and Gavin Hastings. For the rest of the match, English forwards and backs alike hurled themselves at the Scots' line, but in the face of passionate Scottish tackling, spearheaded by the ubiquitous Finlay Calder, they could muster only one Hodgkinson penalty in reply.

After the match, Carling was a target for criticism; in the first half, the English ran some kickable penalties, or opted for scrums, when the direction seemed to be coming not from the England captain, but from his pack leader, Moore.

SCOTLAND: A. G. Hastings (London Scottish); A. G. Stanger (Hawick), S. Hastings (Watsonians), S. R. P. Lineen (Boroughmuir), I. Tukalo (Selkirk); C. M. Chalmers (Melrose), G. Armstrong (Jedforest); D. M. B. Sole (Edinburgh Acads) (*capt*), K. S. Milne (Heriot's FP), A. P. Burnell (London Scottish), C. A. Gray (Nottingham), D. F. Cronin (Bath), J. Jeffrey (Kelso), F. Calder (Stewart's-Melville FP), D. B. White (London Scottish)

Replacement: D. J. Turnbull (Hawick) for White

ENGLAND: S. D. Hodgkinson (Nottingham); S. J. Halliday (Bath), W. D. C. Carling (Harlequins) (*capt*), J. C. Guscott (Bath), R. Underwood (Leicester); C. R. Andrew (Wasps), R. J. Hill

66

(Bath); P. A. G. Rendall (Bath), B. C. Moore (Nottingham),
J. A. Probyn (Wasps), P. J. Ackford (Harlequins), W. A. Dooley
(Preston Grasshoppers), M. G. Skinner (Harlequins),
P. J. Winterbottom (Harlequins), M. C. Teague (Gloucester)

Referee: D. J. Bishop (New Zealand)

Other Match (24 March): IRELAND 14 WALES 8

MONDAY 19 MARCH 1990

I think I have reached a state of mind where I can examine
what happened on Saturday. I was certainly in a state of
shock for twenty-four hours afterwards, and it is only now
that the real pain and sense of loss is coming to bear. The
sadness of the experience comes from having been part of
the side through all the work we have done this year, and
all the time we've given up, all the training we've put in,
as expectations have risen and risen. It is so sad to see that
go to waste, as it has in many people's minds. The media
seem to have forgotten that we played three great games
before we lost the last to a very proud and well-drilled side.
We have come a long way this year and it is a shame that
this side will not get the recognition that I still believe it
deserves.

In the changing room afterwards, all the guys were absolutely shattered: sitting around, their heads in their hands,
with pain and confusion all over their faces. There was

nothing to say. Then we had to endure the criticism afterwards, one of the most painful experiences in sport. Trying to come to terms with the public perception of our defeat is one of the most difficult things I've had to go through. It's been a harrowing two days.

But one of the things I will always remember is the dignified way in which this England squad took the defeat in the course of the evening and the next day. That, I think, is a reflection of their strength of character. I felt privileged then to be involved with them. They could have behaved appallingly in their disappointment, and perhaps been forgiven for it, but they didn't. I'm sure their conduct was appreciated by those who saw it.

So, what went wrong? I think, for a start, the Scots surprised us. Their preparation and their appetite for the game were phenomenal. They were very well organised, and extremely efficient. They moved players in the line-out most intelligently, to counter what we thought would be our advantage there. Their scrummage was stronger than we thought it was going to be. We always knew their defence was going to be tenacious, and it certainly was. Once they got ahead they could close the game up completely, and then they defended with tremendous passion. Critics have said we should have kicked our goals, but at least some of the damage had been done before then. I think we miscalculated the effect of the Scottish crowd; I have never heard support like that in my life, not even at the Arms Park. When the Scots walked out rather than sprinting out in the usual manner, which was a very good psychological ploy by them, it seemed to say that this was the most important game in Scottish rugby history. After that, the crowd never really calmed down, and we couldn't do anything to subdue them. Once the ball is in play, the crowd has no effect on me, but at the start of the game we were certainly very aware of the level of emotion that was flowing round the ground.

As for the game itself: the Scots won the toss and decided to play with the wind, obviously with the intention of getting points on the board. Rob Andrew had said beforehand that our discipline had to be watertight, that we mustn't give them penalties; and in the first minute or two we gave away a silly penalty kick. Then we argued, and the referee moved the kick ten yards nearer the post: 0-3. In the course of the first half we gave away three more kickable penalties for needless offences like rough play, which was unforgivable. We knew that we could compete in the set pieces, and that our defence had been strong all season; the only way the Scots were going to get points on the board early on was through penalty kicks. We handed them their first nine points on a plate, and I think that was the root of our defeat.

A major talking-point has been our not kicking at goal when we had penalties in the right-hand corner in the first half. Some have said that Brian Moore overruled me – that's not true. I wanted to run the ball. The only question was how we ran it. Then, later, we opted for scrums on the line, when we might have got three points through a kick at goal. Well, it would have been a hard kick from the right-hand side, into a strong wind. We were only 6-4 down. We had a pressure position. We had every reason to believe that our strong scrummage could force a pushover try. The Scots' Number 8, Derek White, had injured his knee ligaments and could hardly stand up, so their scrum was effectively down to seven men for that moment and we wanted to take advantage. Besides, there were only ten minutes left of the half, and I wanted to keep the pressure on the Scots. If we'd kicked for goal and missed, they'd have taken a long twenty-two dropout and we'd have been back on our own twenty-two, our stranglehold gone. We'd run penalties in two of the other games we'd played, and we'd got points then – I felt it was still a viable option. And we should have been awarded a penalty try for Sole dropping that scrum on the line – but I guess that's not very relevant any more.

Anyway, though we didn't get the try we were after, the game was far from lost at that stage. We gave away another ridiculous penalty before half-time which made it 9-4, but even so, when we turned round at the interval, I felt we'd done quite well to hold off what was always going to be a very strong Scottish challenge with the wind in the first half – we were still within one strike of gaining the lead. I was confident that we could turn it around.

And the other players seemed to think so, too. We had weathered a fanatical start – the early confrontations between the forwards were gruellingly physical and committed. We'd also scored a great try. We'd got very quick second-phase possession and had opened up the Scottish backs for Jerry Guscott to score; and that was what we wanted to do in the second half, to get down into their twenty-two and put pressure on. But their try early in the second half was a hammer blow – mentally we never came back from it. At 13-4 ahead they realised that they did not have to play constructive rugby any more. They had enough points on the board to win if they could just keep tackling and clearing for half an hour – and they can do that very well, as they showed. In the end we got more and more frantic. We felt the pressure, we weren't as controlled as we would have liked to have been from set pieces and we never really came to terms with the pace of the game that the Scots managed to make us play. At the end we were trying to do everything as quickly as possible, especially round the fringes of the set pieces, which was exactly how they wanted to play it. And the score we needed never came.

It has been said since that, if these two sides had played ten times, England would have won nine times. But knowing we were theoretically the stronger side won't make us feel any better. It certainly wouldn't temper the Scots' celebrations. They got it right on the day, they deserved their win, and they are the 1990 Grand Slam Champions. It is very sad and frustrating for us, as a team and as a group of people, including the management and the medical staff. My own sense of loss is for a dream that has been taken away. Maybe we should never have dreamed that way; but we're only human, and I am sure we all did.

FRIDAY 30 MARCH 1990, HONG KONG

In Hong Kong with the Barbarians, for the sevens tournament. We flew out on Monday night and got here on Tuesday evening, and it's been non-stop since then. The Barbarians, being social animals, wined and dined us at every mealtime. Of course the players have been off the wine, as usual, and the committee men haven't. It's been absolutely great fun here. Hong Kong seems to take a week off, and all the rugby fanatics throw parties: God knows what it's going to be like here tomorrow and on Sunday, which are the days of the actual competition.

It has been very interesting to come across the Australians, the New Zealanders – who have got a very strong side out here – and the Fijians, who have apparently been training since December and who are very keen to avenge their defeats of the last few years. In amongst these are sides such as the West Germans and the Dutch – it's fascinating to meet them all and have a good chat. And of course Hong Kong is an enthralling city. I've been told the place to go to is the hotel massage parlour, where they walk all over your back, but that doesn't really appeal to me.

Tomorrow we've got quite an easy group, I think. We've got West Germany and Canada, although those who've watched Canada in training say they have some very good players, big athletic forwards who play a physical game. Our squad of nine comprises Micky Skinner, Brian Moore, Peter Winterbottom, Richard Moon, Rob Andrew, myself and Jerry Guscott, with Barry Evans and Chris Sheasby. That's a handy line-up; I don't know exactly which seven is going to be selected.

We ought to be able to beat West Germany, and if we overcome Canada as well we'll only be one match away from playing New Zealand in the semi-final. And that would be very interesting.

After the agony of losing to Scotland, it's been something of a relief to come away and play in a completely different environment, and for a side that isn't the national side. There is less pressure, although people over here have got very keen for the Barbarians to do well, because they still look at us as an England side – not surprisingly, considering we have six England internationals. And the disappointment about the lost Grand Slam has penetrated here. I spend much of my time trying to console supporters, which is quite strange. All in all there's a great festive spirit about, although it is hard to marry the fun with playing in the hardest sevens competition in the world. The next two days in this kind of heat, where there's 95 per cent humidity as well, will be very draining indeed, and obviously we haven't had time to acclimatise. But let's see what happens.

THURSDAY 5 APRIL 1990, LONDON

I've flown back from Hong Kong, where I think we did as well as could be expected. We lost in the semi-final to New Zealand, having won our group and beaten Western Samoa in the quarter-finals. A lot of supporters there asked me why England don't fly out and play as a national side. I can see the arguments against: the tournament falls straight after the Five Nations Championship, and we wouldn't be able to compete against New Zealand, Fiji and Australia, who've all been training for three or four weeks just for this event. Also, there are a lot of important club games going on: the Pilkington Cup and league matches. On the other hand, having experienced the wealth of support that there is for England in Hong Kong, it would be nice to give them an authentic national side to cheer on. Still, I would feel frustrated that we didn't have the time to prepare as thoroughly as our opponents.

This was my first contact with New Zealand rugby players on the national level, and I was pleased to talk to the likes of John Gallagher, Zinzan Brooke, Graeme Bachop,

John Schuster and Terry Wright. Their commitment in pursuit of staying the best in the world is awesome. They have total tunnel vision as far as rugby is concerned; the game has dominated their lives since they were six or seven. That's why they're the best. And while I would never want English players to pursue their rugby careers to the exclusion of everything else, it's as well to know the kind of single-mindedness that will be opposing us come the World Cup in eighteen months' time.

To which, after a season which promised everything but gave all the prizes to someone else, we must now begin to turn our thoughts.

PART TWO
1990–91

JULY/AUGUST 1990

The England squad's seven-match tour of Argentina was a depressing coda to a season that had promised so much — or an alarming prelude to the new. England were without six leading players — Andrew, Underwood, Guscott, Richards, Teague and Ackford — and there were some experimental choices in the tour party, but the tour raised doubts about the form of some established internationals and more serious ones about the strength of cover in key positions. England were beaten in the second of the two internationals, and had an even worse record in the provincial matches, losing three out of five.

RESULTS

14 July	Banco Nacion	29	England	21
18 July	Tucuman	14	England	19
21 July	Buenos Aires	26	England	23
24 July	Cujo	22	England	21
28 July	**Argentina**	12	**England**	25
31 July	Cordoba	12	England	15
4 August	**Argentina**	15	**England**	13

TOUR PARTY

Full Backs: S. D. Hodgkinson (Nottingham), J. G. Liley (Leicester)

Wings: N. J. Heslop (Orrell), C. Oti (Wasps), T. Underwood (Leicester)

Centres: J. R. D. Buckton (Saracens), W. D. C. Carling (Harlequins) (*capt.*), C. G. Childs (Northern), G. J. Thompson (Harlequins)

Fly-halves: P. A. Hull (Bristol), D. Pears (Harlequins)

Scrum-halves: R. J. Hill (Bath), C. D. Morris (Orrell)

Props: J. Leonard (Saracens), M. S. Linnett (Moseley), V. E. Ubogu (Bath), J. A. Probyn (Wasps)

Hookers: B. C. Moore (Harlequins), C. J. Olver (Northampton)

Locks: W. A. Dooley (Preston Grasshoppers), R. Kimmins (Orrell), M. D. Poole (Leicester), N. C. Redman (Bath)

Flankers: M. G. Skinner (Harlequins), D. Ryan (Wasps) R. A. Robinson (Bath), P. J. Winterbottom (Harlequins)

Number 8s: D. W. Egerton (Bath), T. A. K. Rodber (Northampton)

Manager: G. D. Cooke
Coach: R. M. Uttley
Physiotherapist: K. Murphy
Doctor: Dr T. Crystal

SATURDAY 11 AUGUST 1990

The whole party was a little apprehensive about going to Argentina. We never really spoke to each other about the possibility of any sort of political problem, but at the back of my mind there was always a doubt about how their public would react to us. When we arrived at the airport and boarded the coach, there were a few policemen around, but nothing too dramatic. Eventually we got into the middle of Buenos Aires and stopped at some traffic lights. We could see the Sheraton Hotel where we were to stay; and a few yards from the hotel was a monument that had obviously just been completed. Under the inscription *Las Malvinas* were engraved the names of all the Argentinian soldiers and sailors who had died in the Falklands war. Again I wondered how much goodwill we could expect on tour. But, in fact, there was never any hint of animosity. Most Argentinians I talked to seemed rather embarrassed about the war. And the hospitality couldn't have been more heartfelt.

Argentina is scenically a very beautiful country, though not as wealthy as her natural resources might lead you to expect. Buenos Aires feels not unlike Paris, with wide boulevards with trees down the middle, but it is sadly run down. Everything needs painting, the roads have got potholes in them. All the cars look about thirty years old, and none of them are insured, because the owners can't afford it; if they have an accident, it's just hard luck.

The facilities in the rugby clubs and the hotels left a bit to be desired. The Sheraton was fine, but when we got out into the towns around the country, standards went down. In one of the hotels we had to share plugs for the bath; in the top hotel in Cordoba the blankets had holes in them. Most of the provincial towns were grey and dull, and yet the people themselves were full of life and fun. The Buenos Aires night-clubs don't get going until two o'clock in the morning. After a game I can very rarely speak at two in the morning, let alone dance. There was the language barrier of course – I think only Richard Hill could speak Spanish. But it seemed to matter less in the early hours of the morning.

Hand signals, the nodding of the head for another drink, and a smile were about all that was needed.

We got on very well with the Argentinian players, and lots of other Argentinians went out of their way for us – one in particular, called Farfar, who was our baggage man. He was about five feet two inches tall, and he prided himself on being able to get us anything we wanted. He would disappear for half a day to try and find a trinket for one of the players: or if we wanted to go shopping, he would take us through little streets to find the best goods and the best prices. We gave him a tracksuit, which he was very proud of, though he had to roll the sleeves up to allow him to use his little hands. He was typical of the way the people made us welcome. They wanted to kick the proverbial out of us while we were playing, and they would rant and rave on the pitch, but afterwards – very like the Fijians after two of them had been sent off! – they were extremely friendly, posing the eternal question about who could drink the most. (It wasn't me).

From a rugby point of view, the tour was a major disappointment. We lost four of our seven matches, including three of the five provincial games – against Banco Nacion (Hugo Porta's club side), the city of Buenos Aires, and Cujo, a district which is apparently not renowned for its rugby strength. Even the games we did win, against Tucuman and Cordoba, were closely-fought (and Cordoba was a fight all right). We certainly underestimated the strength of the provincial sides. They played a simple, hard game, with a lot of kick and chase for backs who tackled very aggressively. Argentina breeds big forwards – not necessarily tall men, but very strong in the upper body, a good advertisement for the effects of steak. They were in the middle of their season, and very fit, and they knocked us out of our stride. We didn't win enough quality ball, and our three-quarters, most of whom were fairly inexperienced, seemed to find it difficult to make the step up to the extra pace and pressure of rugby on an international tour. The trip may have come a little too soon for a few of the younger players; and some of the senior players, perhaps because this had some of the trappings of an 'A' tour, played beneath themselves as well. I know Brian Moore and Wade Dooley were disappointed with their form. Because of our lack of success in the build-up games, we played to a very limited plan in the First Test. We looked to dominate in the line-out and compete in the scrums, and in the backs we didn't look any further than an Argentinian-style kick-and-chase; and it worked. We scored an early try through the back row, by Dean Ryan. We knew their full back liked to run, so we kicked to him and caught him time and again behind his forwards; they gave penalties away, and Simon Hodgkinson kicked them. They never looked like scoring a try, and we pulled away to win quite comfortably.

But the Second Test was a different matter. I think we lacked the necessary desire to win, to be honest – we'd won one, and we were maybe relieved that the tour, which had been hard in some ways, was coming to a close; and on the other hand, the Argentinians saw this as their last chance, and came out with all guns blazing.

Still, we should have won it. We played the same kicking game, while they, to their credit, had evolved a more varied strategy, spinning it wide from the first few minutes and catching us cold. We made mistakes under pressure because we hadn't foreseen that kind of game, and we conceded penalties: they kicked the crucial one in the closing minutes to win the game.

Your first reaction to a tour like that is that it must have done as much harm as good; the results were inescapably

81

awful. But our squad was really terribly young, with fourteen uncapped players, and even those who struggled a little will have taken something from the experience that will help them in the future. And there are more tangible gains, like the form of Nigel Heslop on the wing, some good performances from our back-row reserves, and the emergence of Jason Leonard at prop, who, at twenty-one, could be a real asset in the Championship to come – perhaps even be our loose-head in the World Cup. The chief lesson, however, is that our reserve strength in certain areas, such as fly-half, full back and second-row, is nowhere near good enough at the moment: and woe betide us in the Championship if certain key individuals pick up injuries.

MONDAY 23 AUGUST 1990

I've just got back from a week's holiday in Portugal with my girlfriend, where one or two things happened which reminded me of the difficulties involved in being the captain of England if, like me, you're not naturally an outgoing person. We had this little villa in the hills with its own pool, and we only left the place in the evening to get something to eat. Every night without fail, whichever restaurant we were in, someone would come up to me, ignore my girlfriend and expect me to suspend my meal to hear his views on the game, or to extract mine. Now I'm not the rugby-song type, I don't like large groups of people as a whole, and the attention I get in pubs and restaurants, the pointing and the whispering and the cheerful conversations, is not something I'm at ease with. In fact, I don't really go into pubs any more, for that reason.

Of course I accept that as captain you have a certain amount of duty to the public, which you can best discharge through the press. All the rugby press have my work number and my home number, and as long as they don't pressurise me unreasonably I always try to make myself available to them, and ring them back if I'm out when they call. Then there are the magazine articles, which have attracted a little bit of amused criticism. I did an interview for *GQ* magazine, which was a serious study of rugby and my place in it as England captain. Even though I was on the cover, it wasn't an ego-trip; I'm sure the exercise was basically good for rugby. And I consented to do a thing for the *Mail on Sunday* about health and fitness, which some people perceived as me picking up a plug for myself. But one thing I can do as captain is to try and raise the profile of rugby as a game, and inevitably that will mean accepting some offers that are a bit broader than talking to Chris Rea or Ian Robertson on *Rugby Special*. As a rule I turn down interviews which set their sights on 'the real Will Carling', partly because I value my privacy, partly because I've no wish to be turned into an all-purpose celebrity. I'll do whatever seems to me to tally with the role of captain of England.

That doesn't, incidentally, include swaggering around in public. I'm not one of those who can put their shoulders back when people point and give it the old smug look. I'm also not physically as big as people think! I remember standing in the White Horse pub on Parson's Green, and there was a little hush from one group and one of them came and paused next to me and I sort of caught his eye, and he said: 'I thought you'd be bigger!' He seemed disappointed. So I apologised.

It's important to keep your feet on the ground, and your head under control. I still find it a shock to have little kids asking for my autograph; it reminds me of the responsibility we've got as international players, but I hope it never makes me think that I'm anything special as a human being.

THURSDAY 27 SEPTEMBER 1990

Our early work for the 1991 Championship centres on two big games: next Saturday's against the Barbarians (part of their centenary celebrations) and the home international against Argentina on 2 November. After the mishaps against Scotland in March and in Argentina, it's vital that we recover our momentum in these games, or some of the squad will drift out of international rugby as under-achievers. And although the Barbarians are, as always, a scratch side, they have a dozen world-class players who will be determined to beat England. They'll have Campese and Lafond on the wings, two of the best broken-field runners in the world; the Australian half-backs, Farr-Jones and Lynagh; and two huge locks, the new All Black Ian Jones and Steve Cutler (who has a point to prove to the Australian selectors), who'll test Ackford and Dooley's claim to be the best line-out pairing in the world. Many of their players will just have finished their season in the

The team that won the Grand Slam: England v France, 16 March 1991

STANDING, FROM LEFT: Derek Bevan (Touch Judge); Geoff Cooke (Manager); Simon Halliday, Jonathan Webb (Replacements); Rory Underwood, Peter Winterbottom, Mike Teague, Paul Ackford, Wade Dooley, Dean Richards, Jeff Probyn, Jason Leonard; Mick Skinner, Dewi Morris (Replacements); Roger Uttley (Coach); Clive Norling (Touch Judge)

SEATED: Paul Rendall (Replacement); Nigel Heslop, Brian Moore, Richard Hill, Will Carling (Captain), Rob Andrew, Jeremy Guscott, Simon Hodgkinson; John Olver (Replacement)

The Front Row: Probyn, Moore, Leonard

The Back Row: Teague, Richards, Winterbottom

Paul Ackford

Wade Dooley

Richard Hill

Rob Andrew

ory Underwood

Simon Hodgkinson

WALES *v* ENGLAND 1991

TOP Dean Richards charges the Welsh midfield BOTTOM Simon Hodgkinson's seventh successful penalty breaks the world record

ENGLAND *v* SCOTLAND 1991

Paul Ackford gets the better of Chris Gray in another line-out

IRELAND *v* ENGLAND 1991

TOP The breakthrough: Rory Underwood bursts for the line with seven minutes remaining
BOTTOM Mike Teague celebrates the second try

ENGLAND *v* FRANCE 1991

TOP LEFT I look on while Teague and Winterbottom stifle Blanco TOP RIGHT A prayer and a
wing: I look for guidance while BOTTOM Rory Underwood scorches in for his first-half try

The Grand Slam is Ours! TOP the final whistle blows BOTTOM fans chair me off the pitch

Southern Hemisphere, so they ought to be at peak fitness. We had a hard session last weekend, and we're preparing for this as the first of six international outings in the new campaign. The Barbarians may want to turn it into an exhibition match; we'll want to keep things as tight as we can. It will be interesting to see which method will prevail.

SUNDAY 30 SEPTEMBER 1990

We beat the Barbarians in good style, even if without much to spare: 18–16. They scored a memorable try in the second half, when they took a short penalty in their own half and sent Eric Rush, the Auckland flanker, haring through the middle; he made a huge dent and then the ball went left, with substitute flanker and England B player Neil Back handling twice before the Number 8 Phil Davies scored in the corner.

But for most of the rest of the game we were in control. Dooley and Ackford ruled the line-out, where we introduced some variations, switching the jumpers and using a shortened line. In the scrum, where Jason Leonard was making his first Twickenham appearance for England, in opposition to the All Black Richard Loe, we creaked a bit for the first twenty minutes, but for the rest of the match we were very solid. Secure in the set pieces, we were able to launch our driving, rolling mauls at them, sapping their energy and tying them in. We played to our strengths and

executed the forward drills that as a scratch side they couldn't match. Our line-out advantage meant that we could play the touchlines.

I'm relieved to have won, and satisfied by the way we played. It's not the prettiest brand of rugby, but it might just be the method that will see us through this year's Championship. The next test of it will come in just over a month's time, when we have the chance to get our own back against Argentina.

SATURDAY 3 NOVEMBER 1990, TWICKENHAM

ENGLAND 51   **ARGENTINA 0**

Tries: Hill
                  Underwood (3)
                  Guscott (2)
                  Hall

Conversions: Hodgkinson (7)

Penalties: Hodgkinson (3)

This was England's highest score without reply in international matches, and their fourth highest total in all, and Simon Hodgkinson's 23 points were a record for an individual Englishman in an international. But the record-breaking, and the grinding power of England's forward play, were partially overshadowed by the vicious punch which earned the 18-year-old Argentinian prop, Federico Mendez, his marching orders.

England were 15-0 up after only a quarter of an hour, and in that first period Argentina were deprived of a single worthwhile piece of possession. When the rugged tackling of Allen began to disrupt England's midfield moves, they switched the emphasis in attack to the back row, where John Hall made a forceful return to international rugby, and scrum-half Hill, who enjoyed a luxurious afternoon

*behind his steamroller pack. Left-winger Underwood was
another to revel in the amount of space that was won for
him to run in.*

*The score was 33-0 when Mendez lost his head, tangled
with his opposite number, Probyn, then laid out Paul Ackford with a haymaker from behind.*

ENGLAND: S. D. Hodgkinson (Nottingham); N. J. Heslop
(Orrell), W. D. C. Carling (Harlequins) (*capt.*), J. C. Guscott (Bath),
R. Underwood (Leicester); C. R. Andrew (Wasps), R. J. Hill (Bath);
J. Leonard (Harlequins), C. J. Olver, (Northampton), J. A. Probyn
(Wasps), P. J. Ackford (Harlequins), W. A. Dooley (Preston
Grasshoppers), J. P. Hall (Bath), P. J. Winterbottom (Harlequins),
Dean Richards (Leicester)

Replacement: G. W. Rees (Nottingham) for Ackford

ARGENTINA: A. A. Scolni; S. Excurra, D. Cuesta Silva, M.
Allen, G. M. Jorge; H. Porta (*capt.*), G. Camardon; F. E. Mendez,
R. A. Le Fort, D. M. Cash, G. Llanes, P. Sporleder, P. A. Garreton,
M. J. S. Bertranou, A. M. Macombe

Sent Off: Mendez

Referee: C. J. Hawke (New Zealand)

SUNDAY 4 NOVEMBER 1990

Revenge is sweet, and we really enjoyed taking this Argentina side apart. Even the guys who hadn't been on the
summer tour, like Rob Andrew and Paul Ackford, had been
hurt by the criticism that our play over there had attracted,

especially as it came after the terrible disappointment of defeat at Murrayfield. So the feeling was – right, a new season, let's show people what we can do; and let's start with the opponents who embarrassed us three months ago. And without disrespect to the young tourists, there was a sense at last weekend's squad session of the real England being back together, a team that could show Argentina the full strength of our national side. There were just a couple of changes from the side that beat the Barbarians: Nigel Heslop came in for Tony Underwood, and John Hall, who's back to full fitness and had been playing very powerfully for Bath, came in on the blind side in place of Mike Teague.

We expected to do well in the line-out, and the plan was to spin that possession wide and let our runners loose. The Argentinians hadn't seen Rob or Jerry or Rory on tour, and they had no answer to runners of that class. As we had, Argentina had brought over a young side, and they were perhaps as underpowered in our country as we had been in theirs; but this was the side that very nearly beat Ireland a few days ago, so we didn't anticipate a rout. In the event, for the first twenty minutes of the game they hardly touched the ball, we had such a stranglehold. In fact we managed to retain the ball very well throughout, the thing we'd failed to do in Argentina.

And then there was the punch, which has tended to monopolise the media response to the game, as the occasional flashpoints of violence in international matches invariably do.

In a highly physical sport like rugby, which puts players into vigorous contact with each other, there are always going to be moments of frustration or annoyance when people lash out spontaneously. I don't say they're right to do so, but most 'punches' of that sort are just clumsy reflex actions, most of them don't land, and very few of them

89

hurt. They're an understandable if unsightly part of the game. But the punch by Mendez, their schoolboy prop, was a different kind of thing. It began when Mendez grabbed Jeff Probyn's groin, and Jeff retaliated by stamping on him. Mendez then got up determined to hit someone, and lined up Paul Ackford, a completely innocent party who happened to be looking the other way and so couldn't ride the blow. It was a dangerous assault, and the fact that he was sent off, that his side was punished for his actions, doesn't diminish the damage that this sort of incident does to the game.

Likewise, everyone accepts the rucking of a player on the ground who's blocking release of the ball as a legitimate part of the game. What we can't condone and what referees must never allow is stamping on players to hurt them, and especially stamping on the head. I'm glad that referee Fred Howard has helped establish this as a sending-off offence, offering the early bath to Kevin Moseley of Wales and Alain Carminati of France in last season's Championship. Players don't want violence, and as long as referees are tough they're glad to get on with the game. It's when referees let the offenders go unpunished that problems begin to occur.

There have been occasions when a team has been psyched up to intimidate opponents not by hard tackling and rucking and mauling, but with the fist and the boot. Teams like that don't *frighten* people – certainly not an international level, where a scared forward is a thing you'll never see. But it makes for unpleasant games; if the referee doesn't intervene, players have to act to protect themselves. It's unrealistic and dangerous to expect them to turn the other cheek. (That's literally what Sandy Carmichael of the British Lions did against the punchers of Canterbury in 1971; and he ended up with two broken cheekbones.) The current England side won't sit still and be kicked around; but they're mature enough to concentrate on the rugby. And I like to think we have a good disciplinary record by now.

I've come across a few players who you know will try and stamp on you if they can catch you on the floor, or gouge your eyes if you're stuck in a maul. A couple of current Welsh international forwards spring to mind. Some French forwards are tricky, but from them it's only an extension of their club rugby, which is the most brutal in the world – you don't feel that the violence is directed against you personally. But those Welsh forwards I mentioned go in to maim individuals, and everyone knows what they're up to. Again, they rarely hurt you – Mike Teague having his head split open in the first seconds of our 1989 game at Cardiff was an exception. But you look at these blokes as you leave the pitch and think, Do I really have to drink with you tonight? – which is a shame.

The really hard men, needless to say, don't have to bother with that sort of thing: though they will be teasing Paul Ackford next week about being knocked out by a schoolboy.

SUNDAY 2 DECEMBER 1990

The first three Saturdays of December are given over to the Divisional Championship. While that means consistently hard rugby, it also means I ought to be able to relax a little out of the limelight until preparations for the Home Championship gather momentum. But not a bit of it.

This has been a terrible week for me. On Monday I wrote my Mercedes off in an accident; and the police reckon it was my fault. I was driving back from training with the London team, and I'd been talking with the coach Dick Best for about an hour afterwards. So it was about half past eleven when I was coming down the A316, and it was pouring with rain. I drew up at some lights next to two young blokes in a sports car. As we pulled away they cut me up, and when I braked the tail of my car flipped round and I ended up going backwards down the wrong side of the road. I hit two cars.

To my great relief, no one was seriously hurt. One chap had a slight cut to his head, the other had a sore foot, and I was pretty shaken up. But I was very lucky. I must have come close to killing someone, not least myself; as I was going backwards it certainly occurred to me that this was it.

Then, just as I was getting over the shock of the accident, I went down on Thursday to speak at a conference. All sorts of questions, about football, Paul Gascoigne, and a lot else, and I made some impromptu comments. On Friday there were banner headlines in the papers about how I had slated Gazza and the game of football, this, that and the other. And now to cap it all there are allegations in another paper that I have received payment for opening a sports complex. And I have been asked to produce documentation to prove that I didn't. I seem to be identified by some of those who want to preserve rugby's amateur ethos with the changes that are inevitably coming into the game. I would remind them that people have been clamouring for a change in rugby since I started reading about it. The likes of Fran Cotton and Steve Smith were arguing back in the seventies that amateurism couldn't be maintained. The Southern Hemisphere countries have long been pushing hard for changes in the rules; I'm sure no one there regards me as a ringleader!

Anyway, what has happened in this case is that someone wrote to the RFU complaining that I had infringed the amateur regulations; and Dudley Eggar replied that if the man had evidence, then the RFU would take action. So the guy sends back an invoice and a letter, and he sends them to the press as well. At no stage has he rung me or asked me for my explanation. I have explained everything to the Rugby Union, that the fee went to charity, etc. But the consequence of this man's actions is that a certain reporter is currently ringing round rugby clubs and other places to see whether I have done any speaking for them, and whether I got paid for it. The whole thing seems to me to be getting out of hand.

There's another accusation doing the rounds: that I have only set up my company in management and leadership training because I am captain of England. But I've always been interested in leadership – that's why I joined the army.

I read psychology at Durham University, because I was fascinated by what made people tick and why certain people performed better than others. And I have always enjoyed captaining sides, and now I am lucky enough to have been made captain of England. No doubt that's been a great help to me in getting my business going. But it is something that I have always wanted to do. It is not a front for brown paper envelopes for Will Carling, or for me to promote myself. In fact, I could easily promote myself within the regulations: there's nothing to stop me setting up Will Carling Incorporated if I want to. But I don't. I just hope all this dies down fairly soon, so that we can clear our minds for the Five Nations.

After a week like that I enjoyed the Divisional game yesterday – London against the North. We won pretty heavily. I felt happy with my game, and I scored at the end, which was, I think, useful in showing the press that I can still function on the field. I feel at the moment that I never want to read another newspaper, and I'm growing suspicious of the motives of anyone who wants to know my views; and yet I don't suppose I have come across anything resembling the intrusions that the likes of Botham, Gascoigne, and Daley Thompson have had to endure. Rugby players still seem to get off lightly, overall; not that I feel the privilege, at the moment.

But all is not glum. And although my ankle is a bit sore, and I'm doubtful for next Saturday, I'm sure I will be playing again before the end of the Divisionals and, once I get out on the pitch, I know I'll enjoy being a rugby player again.

MONDAY 17 DECEMBER 1990

Well, things haven't improved. In fact, with the furore surrounding my being dropped from the London side, they've got worse.

Near the end of our first Divisional game against the North I felt something go in my ankle. I played on, but by the evening it was really sore, and the pain woke me up every night for a week. The tendon that runs down to the big toe had been damaged.

So I missed the second Divisional game last weekend, in which London narrowly beat the Midlands, 25–24. I was picked for the last game, against the South-West, although my injury was still troubling me on the Tuesday. There was training on Thursday, which I couldn't get to, because I was delayed on business in Glasgow. For one reason or another, I didn't phone Graham Smith, the chairman of the London selectors, to tell him I'd miss training – he found out through Rob Andrew, who's captain of the London side, but felt this wasn't good enough, and pronounced me dropped on Thursday night.

I can see I handled things poorly. I was very keen to play if my ankle had permitted, and I'm not the sort to skip training on a whim. So I feel I've been misunderstood. On the other hand, I could have averted all this with a phone call, so I've only got myself to blame. In extenuation, I've had a hard month of criticism in the press, of having to answer in public allegations that have been made to the RFU in private – I do think the RFU have dealt unfairly there – and precious little rugby. I've been talking a lot recently to Rob Andrew, who coped so well when the press were crucifying him three or four years ago. He's been a great help, advising me just to get my head down, play my best and wait for them to find another target. My problem is that the press have had me in their sights while I've been injured. The only statement you can usefully make as a rugby player is on the pitch, and that hasn't been available to me.

And unfortunately the London business has meant another round of media attention. I turned up to watch the game at Gloucester on Saturday, not only to keep face but because I wanted to be there; and again the cameras were trained on me. And in yesterday's *Independent on Sunday* there was speculation from Chris Rea that I'm going to resign as England captain. I don't know where he got that one from, and it couldn't be further from the truth. This latest business hasn't affected my status in the England set-up. Geoff Cooke rang me to see what had gone wrong, and is satisfied with my explanation. He knows me too well to think I would just arrogantly miss training because I didn't fancy it.

Anyway, I'm glad Christmas is upon us. I'll be spending four or five days with my parents and grandparents in the family home in Clapham. My brother Marcus will be over from Hong Kong, where he's stationed in the army – he's a captain in the Royal Regiment of Wales. I like to let off steam with him. He's a good rugby player himself – he's played for the Colony – but has a more social view of the game than I do, and likes to have a bloody good time while he's at it. He follows my progress very carefully; he's pleased for me, but he's very unimpressed by all the hype.

And then in the New Year the squad will have five days in Lanzarote, where we can put 1990 behind us – and I can put this last month behind me – and look forward to the Championship. It's a nice thought that the media will have some rugby to concentrate on, too.

TUESDAY 8 JANUARY 1991

Back from Lanzarote, after five really constructive days. On the Friday and the Saturday we had sixty minutes of actual playing which was as committed as any rugby I've played for a while. It's cheering to watch people like Peter Winterbottom tackle so hard and put so much energy in, when he must know that his position is not in doubt for the first international. If you were caught on the floor in those sessions you expected to get a raking, but we all went out in the evening and enjoyed a meal together. It's no longer something to be ashamed of, to want to do well, and the cynicism around the England set-up that I had heard about when I first got into the squad is definitely a thing of the past.

The only minus to come out of this trip is that John Hall has injured his knee. How serious this is we don't know yet. But at least we have great cover for his position. If Hall isn't fit, Mike Teague will take his place, and Micky

Skinner will be on the bench. We're very lucky to have three players of that calibre vying for the blind-side flanker's role. (Mike Teague's fitness, incidentally, is remarkable; he has been working phenomenally hard, and it's difficult to contemplate that someone with so much determination might not even make the side.) Hard to say which of the three would perform better in Cardiff; they have three such distinctive styles. The state of John Hall's knee will make the decision for us.

I had the usual press conference grilling out there, alongside Geoff Cooke. We spent nearly half an hour on the subject of whether or not there was an alcohol ban on players. And these were experienced journalists. It was a bit like being at school. I was cross-examined about the events of the last couple of months, and it took me ten minutes to convince members of the press that I would say nothing more than 'What is behind me is behind me, I'm looking forward to the Five Nations, and training hard for it.' They are amazingly persistent.

SUNDAY 13 JANUARY 1991

John Hall is definitely out; he's had a cartilage operation. Mr Bliss, the surgeon down at the Bath Clinic, expects him to be up and running in a matter of days; he doesn't think the damage is too severe, just abnormalities (whatever that means). It's good news really, that, although he is out of this game, he will be back in contention sooner than people expected. For the time being, at any rate, we've got Mike Teague on the blind-side flank, and I'm very happy with that.

In today's squad session at Twickenham, England played England B under the refereeing of Dick Best. It was meant to be a 50 per cent session, but certain players were going all out, and by the end there were a few frayed tempers around. Perhaps that's not such a bad thing. I remember that the preparation before the Scottish game last year was one of the smoothest we had ever had. But we play Wales in six days' time, and it was disconcerting that things should have degenerated so quickly after Lanzarote.

THURSDAY 17 JANUARY 1991, THE CREST HOTEL, CARDIFF

My room overlooks the Cardiff club ground; the Arms Park is just behind it, and the floodlights are on. I assume the Welsh team are training there tonight. We arrived two hours ago by coach, and I was joking about the friendliness of the Welsh with Damian Hopley, the young Wasps centre who's come in as our three-quarter replacement. We got off the coach and were just unloading our bags when a Transit van went past honking its horn, and there was the old driver desperately giving it the two fingers – a typical 'Welcome to Cardiff'. It reminded us again just how much the game matters to people in both countries. There's something special for the Welsh taking on England at the Arms Park – the whole nation goes fanatical.

When it comes to games like this, international rugby bears no relation to the sport we all start playing for fun. It's become so important to so many people, and in a perverse kind of way I wouldn't have it otherwise. I love the pressure, yet at the same time I'd love to be able to play without it. You can't have it both ways, of course.

There's been the usual hype. For this match the big thing has been the twenty-eight-year bogey – England last won in Cardiff in 1963. Of course, all that history is irrelevant to me. I've been here once before, when we lost, and that's as far as the 'bogey' runs for me. Gerald Davies said, two years ago, that it was foolish to pretend that Wales-England is just another game; but I swear I have as much desire to beat the Scots at Murrayfield, to beat the French in Paris, and to beat the Irish in Dublin. I want to beat them all. But Saturday's game is important for other reasons. As well as the first game of this year's Championship, it's the first game of our World Cup year; the first of the eleven or twelve internationals we'll play this year, and we've got to get off on the right foot.

We had a session this morning, running through our short penalty ploys and line-out variations. The backs went through some moves, but it wasn't particularly tidy. Rob Andrew came up to me at the end and asked how I felt the atmosphere was. It didn't seem to me to be quite good enough. I talked to the pack and they said that we were still two days off the game and we couldn't expect to come to the boil now and maintain it for two days. We're all agreed, though, that we need a powerful meeting tonight to start raising the adrenalin and to focus our minds on what has to happen on Saturday.

I had lunch with Alan Jones, the Australian coach, before Christmas, and he was talking about this game and how I should approach it. He said: 'If I were in your position I would say to them, "The whole world considers England as one of the best sides around now, yet there is a question mark over whether we have got the hardness, the steel to win the Big Game. We are perceived to have failed twice when it really mattered." ' I don't necessarily go along with that. Paris last year was as big a game as you could get. But perhaps we do have that point to prove. I want us to come away on Sunday saying, 'Yes, we're a good side. And mentally we're hard as nails.'

FRIDAY 18 JANUARY 1991: 5.45 P.M.

We trained again this morning and although we dropped three balls – the usual index of the success of a session – it wasn't as bad as that would suggest. We were speeding things up pretty well by the end. Last night we had a long, thoughtful meeting. We decided that we wanted to take the initiative from the kick-off; it we win the toss, we will kick short right, having split the forwards, which I hope will startle the Welsh right from the word go. They'll be very psyched-up and looking for straightforward confrontation early on – instead they're going to have to do some thinking and adapting.

FRIDAY 18 JANUARY 1991:
MIDNIGHT

Looking out of my window at the black silhouette of the Arms Park. I involved four or five of the players in tonight's meeting, just to get some different views. It was a very tight and intense discussion. The major theme was our need to establish an early initiative in the game – always so hard to do in internationals, where your opponents are always just as committed as you. That initiative isn't necessarily a matter of points or territory. It's in the mind. It's getting the first hits. It happened for us last year in the first scrum, when we demolished them.

We've done all the preparation, and now maybe we just need our share of the luck. You can concentrate and make sure you do the basics properly, but you can't foretell the bounce of the ball. If we get our share of the luck, however, we ought to win tomorrow.

SATURDAY 19 JANUARY 1991, CARDIFF ARMS PARK

WALES 6   **ENGLAND** 25

Penalties: Thorburn   **Try:**   Teague

           Jenkins   **Penalties:** Hodgkinson (7)

England duly recorded their first win in Cardiff for twenty-eight years, and their largest win ever in Wales, but the game itself was not one to get excited about. All but four of England's points came from penalty kicks; Hodgkinson's total of seven was a new world record. The inexperienced Welsh forwards were unable to resist their powerful English counterparts other than by infringements, which Hodgkinson repeatedly punished. Mike Teague relieved the pattern by scoring a try from a five-metre scrum to cap an outstanding personal performance.

Will Carling and the England management caused a stir after the game by boycotting the press conference, a move which was confused in some quarters with the squad's dispute with the BBC over a fee that their agent had sought for post-match interviews.

WALES: P. H. Thorburn (Neath) (*capt*); I. C. Evans (Llanelli), M. G. Ring (Cardiff), I. S. Gibbs (Neath), S. P. Ford (Cardiff), N. R. Jenkins (Pontypridd), R. N. Jones (Swansea); B. R. Williams (Neath), K. H. Phillips (Neath), P. Knight (Pontypridd),

103

G. D. Llewellyn (Neath), G. O. Llewellyn (Neath), A. J. Carter (Newport), G. M. George (Newport), P. Arnold (Swansea)

ENGLAND: S. D. Hodgkinson (Nottingham); N. J. Heslop (Orrell), W. D. C. Carling (Harlequins) (*capt*), J. C. Guscott (Bath), R. Underwood (Leicester); C. R. Andrew (Wasps), R. J. Hill (Bath); J. Leonard (Harlequins), B. C. Moore (Harlequins), J. A. Probyn (Wasps), P. J. Ackford (Harlequins), W. A. Dooley (Preston Grasshoppers), M. C. Teague (Gloucester), P. J. Winterbottom (Harlequins), D. Richards (Leicester)

Referee: R. Megson (Scotland)

Other Match: FRANCE   15   SCOTLAND   9

SATURDAY 19 JANUARY 1991: 6 P.M.

Eighteen hours later, and it's all dark again. The stadium is quiet and deserted, apart from a few groups still at it in the hospitality boxes.

I've got slightly mixed feelings about today's game. Part of me wishes we could have played a more spectacular game – throwing it around as we did last year. But you have to be realistic. I have never played in a game which was so tense from our point of view; after Scotland last year, I don't know how I would have come to terms with losing again. For now, I'm satisfied to have got the right result. We did enough well. We mauled powerfully. Communications between scrum-half, fly-half and the forwards were good. Our tactical kicking was excellent. And Simon

Hodgkinson's goalkicking was astonishing; his total of seven penalties is a new world record.

Our control was more or less constant. At half-time we were 12-3 up, having eased off in the last fifteen minutes. They had their best spell of the match at the beginning of the second half, but we weathered that and came back to play a very tight game, camped in their half. Richard Hill was kicking into the box, and the forwards were driving a lot. When Rob didn't kick, he popped it to Jerry and me, and we would bring it back to the forwards. We wanted to keep it close to the likes of Dean Richards and Mike Teague, who could out-maul their opponents. Eventually, we ground them down and scored a try from a five-metre scrum. Not much of a spectacle, maybe, but you've got to understand the tension of the occasion.

For the first time ever, we walked to the ground from our hotel, four hundred yards away. Until this year, visiting England teams had stayed in a quiet country hotel near Chepstow. But Geoff thought we should build up for this one in the shadow of the stadium, as if to symbolise a new approach.

Once in the stadium we had our usual stroll on the pitch. The surface was good, but with the rain we'd had it was fairly greasy on top. This confirmed for Rob and me that we should keep things tight early on. We had much the more experienced pack – their forwards had very few caps between them – only one cap in the back row – so we wanted to inflict as much pressure as possible early on, and to make sure there would be a lot of set-pieces. So kicking was to be the order of the day, using the three-quarters mainly to set up second-phase situations.

We were in the changing room a little longer than usual – about an hour and a half. As usual, Rory sat in his blazer and tie until about forty minutes before kick-off. Dean took the forwards away, about twenty-five minutes before kick-off, into the showers, and warmed them up in there. And then we were running out of the tunnel. Some of our older players have said they didn't feel that there was the usual fanaticism and noise you expect from an Arms Park crowd. Maybe that helped us. During the anthems I looked down the line at the teams and I realised that the Welsh boys were more daunted than we were.

We kicked off short, as planned, but soon we'd given a couple of penalties away, and Thorburn kicked one of them for three points after three minutes. Not a great start; but even amid the clamour, I knew we'd soon be in our stride – I knew we wouldn't lose. I got tremendous confidence from our back row of Richards, Teague, and Winterbottom. They have played international rugby for many years, and the new Welsh back row were always going to struggle in the physical confrontation and in the reading of the game.

Thorburn began to miss his kicks, which was rare for him. When he missed for the second time you could sense the deflation among the crowd as well as the Welsh players – as if, with their kicker off form, their last hope had gone. That was probably only twenty minutes into the game, but the die was cast. After that, though we didn't play very ambitiously, we still gave Wales their heaviest-ever defeat at the Arms Park.

The atmosphere in the changing room afterwards was a bit subdued. A few of the players were annoyed with themselves, thinking they hadn't played well – Dean, who'd made some errors, was down in the dumps. And there was a sense of anticlimax because it hadn't been as hard a game as we'd expected, even though the Welsh played well in parts.

We didn't speak to the press after the game. That decision

was made in the changing room, and it was nothing to do with money. We'd been frustrated by the activities of certain pressmen who'd been ringing players up at home at all hours of the day and night, and banging on doors for interviews. Some days I get fifteen or twenty calls from members of the media, and I know Rob gets something similar, and when you're trying to work as well that's a real burden. We felt that there had to be some code of conduct which meant that rugby players would not be hounded twenty-four hours a day. It doesn't happen in other sports, and I don't see any reason why England rugby players should be open to that sort of harassment. I regret that it may have seemed a churlish reaction at the time, but something had to be done. We also need protection in the build-up to internationals. We shouldn't have pressmen trying to sneak into the hotel to catch players off their guard. This isn't a grudge against the press in general. I think the press, too, would like to know what the rules of engagement are, and then both sides can play by those rules and keep the relationship healthy.

Anyway, I think the RFU will now be aware of the situation, and they will have to draw up some guidelines for the press, which will govern the internationals themselves and the time between internationals when players are trying to earn their living and pay back the employers who give them so much time off.

MONDAY 28 JANUARY 1991

Another round of Pilkington Cup games negotiated without injuries, as far as I can gather. We're planning to have a squad get-together this weekend when we'll analyse the Scotland-Wales game on TV and video to prepare us for Scotland two weeks after that. It is hard to keep momentum going when you have a game off in the Five Nations; it cost us dear last year. On the other hand, it's a useful breather; it's allowed John Hall to get over his knee problem, and he's back in the squad, as are John Buckton and Simon Halliday. So we are slowly getting over our injuries; the only man still missing from the squad is Chris Oti.

The Scots will pose completely different problems from the Welsh. From the video of their game in Paris, they're still predominantly using a kicking game, with Chalmers standing very deep behind his pack and hoisting the ball high, usually to the centre. Sean Lineen and Scott Hastings, who are excellent chasers, pincer in on it, with the back row moving in very quickly. They still play the ten-metre rule very well, and we've got to come to terms with that. Counter-attacking is not exactly an English forte, but is something which I think we could work on usefully in the next three weeks. We can also draw some encouragement from the fact that the Scots will be without Finlay Calder, who was their outstanding player at Murrayfield last year, and an awkward, irrepressible opponent at all times, fast and hard and full of chat and guile.

MONDAY 4 FEBRUARY 1991

Just another day in the office. My company, Inspirational Horizons, organises conferences, using sport as a metaphor for business and involving top sportsmen in our presentations. At the moment we're putting together a package with Gary Lineker and David Gower. We're also working on a day-long package: four big names will come in and take part in proper scripted presentations about motivation, team management, subjects like that. This isn't just a chance to rub shoulders with Gary Lineker over lunch. Sport seems to elicit an emotional response from businessmen; and if you have sportsmen putting across a serious message as well, you have the recipe for a memorable presentation.

What you notice about top sportsmen is how (with a few famous exceptions) they take it for granted that they have to organise themselves properly. They know they have to peak at a certain time, and they plan for that. Unfortunately, those in other fields don't often organise themselves in such a way, though the peaks of their working 'season' are just as easy to identify.

The idea germinated while I was working for Mobil. They had a big conference in Monte Carlo, with two thousand attending and ten speakers. There were experts of all

109

sorts, but the speaker who really caught the imagination was Frank Dick, the athletics coach. His presentation incorporated videos of Steve Cram, Daley Thompson and others. His theme was the difference between Hill People, who want to move up, and Valley People, who want to stay where they are. It suddenly struck me that there was a real opportunity for the marketing of sportsmen within business.

Of course my contribution flags a bit when the Championship's in progress. (It flags even more when I'm on tour.) Like all amateur sportsmen, I find the dual responsibility difficult. From January to March, I tend to limit myself to the vital meetings. I suppose one of the advantages of being England captain is that it tends to get me quick access to the people in a company who make the decisions. This might look like exploiting my position, but I can hardly be expected to be a shrinking violet at work because of that. It's a worthwhile business that will carry on long after I've finished playing; and it isn't a matter of touring the country opening factories.

I usually get up around seven and get down to the gym for an hour-and-a-half's training of one kind or another. I arrive at the office between nine-thirty and ten, and pick up messages from the press. There are at least four or five of these a day, and replying to them eats away at my mornings. Lunch will usually be business, discussing either a forthcoming presentation or perhaps a long-term project. There'll be one or two meetings in the afternoon, either to get information on a company – the structure its employees work in, and so on – or to fix venues and numbers for a conference. I get away between five and six. If there's no training at Harlequins, I'll try to see a friend or two.

But this schedule tends to go out of the window during the Five Nations Championship. I could easily spend all day, every day for two months on the phone to the press, and that obviously wouldn't be good enough given my place in the company. That's the strain – trying to be polite, and to live up to the public's expectation of an accessible England captain, and at the same time meeting my responsibilities at work.

Dealing with the press is one aspect of the captain's role that I'm not altogether at ease with. I have to weigh my public duties carefully against an instinctive desire to put my head in a dark room and forget about it. I try to speak to all the rugby correspondents: some of them I trust as individuals, others I've become wary of; but friendship is not really possible, as you've got to accept their criticism. Most of the broadsheet writers are fair, and I can talk to them off the record; and I get on pretty well with Tony Roche of *Today*.

I'm getting some pretty strange treatment from Chris Rea at the moment – he writes for the *Independent on Sunday* and presents *Rugby Special*. He announced last month that I was going to give up the captaincy, and really flogged this line without ever contacting me to sample my views on the subject. I never had any intention of resigning. And he's not been in contact since. I don't know whether he thinks he's blundered, or not. But I've not heard a word.

At least we've been spared – up to now – the more prurient sort of attention that the tabloids give to the private lives of footballers and a few cricketers. The boys from the tabloids ask often enough who my girlfriend is, whether we're going to get married, where do we go when we're out, and so on – it's starting to happen more and more. But as far as I'm concerned my girlfriend is my business. I've no intention of parading her in public, and she wants none of it either. I just don't see it as part of my duty as captain; after all, she doesn't play for England (there, that rules out Wade Dooley).

Anyway, the pressure will be off a little for a few days, as our next international is in a month's time, against Scotland at home.

THURSDAY 14 FEBRUARY 1991

There's been a lot of talk lately about the amateur regulations, and about the confrontation between the players and the RFU, in the person of Dudley Woods. The press conference which Geoff Cooke and I gave today was dominated by questions on the issue, and what effect it might be having on the players. From the players' point of view, it could never by anything, in the middle of the Five Nations Championship, other than a side issue. The two-month campaign is so claustrophobic and intense that you have very little time to think about anything else; and those who think that an England team might be motivated by the chance of financial reward are very wide of the mark. At the moment, all we are thinking about is playing Scotland, then Ireland, then France. The other matter can be sorted out some other time. That's the players' feeling. As for the RFU, I really couldn't say. Certain individuals seem to be getting emotional about what's happening, but they'll have to accept that the game is changing, and help to get things resolved sensibly, and sooner rather than later. We are moving into an era when rugby union will have to start selling itself aggressively to youngsters – otherwise no one will take the game up. Marketing the top players will be an important part of that. At the moment, there's a bit of paranoia being generated by the idea of *money* – and that really is not the issue as far as I am concerned. It's the profile of the game and its appeal in the future that we've got to work on.

And so to the Scotland game. This has been characterised as a revenge match, which might be a little too simple. It's a new season, and this game comes at a different stage in the Championship, and we're playing at Twickenham, not Murrayfield. But I can't deny that what happened last year will be a major part of our motivation for this one. It still hurts me to remember the scene in our changing room at Murrayfield, the boys all so dejected. The Scots played extremely well – they'd prepared very thoroughly, and the game went almost exactly as they would have wanted it to. And so they, not us, are known as the 1990 Grand Slam winners. That is a tremendous psychological spur for us. This evening Geoff Cooke, Rob Andrew and I talked for a while about the mental state of the players; but it's quite hard to gauge as early as the Thursday how they're shaping up.

There are certain players who like to stay as relaxed as possible, and save all their emotional energy for the day itself. Others need to feel the adrenalin building up throughout the week. There are not going to be any motivational problems. My main concern is to make sure that we keep our concentration, that we don't go out and play at a hundred miles an hour without the necessary discipline.

Where I think we must make up some ground is in our speed of reaction. We are a very good set-piece side; our pack is tremendously powerful in the scrum and line-out.

But what we have to admit is that the Scots pack are faster than us as a unit; they move quicker, and they seem to react a little quicker than us. In poundage and power we have the edge: but we've got to get to the breakdowns quickly enough to make that advantage count. I'm sure we can react more quickly; we were in such control against Wales that our speed of thought wasn't tested. It will be on Saturday. The Scots will want to play the game at pace, and move the ball away from the set-pieces. A lot will depend on how quickly our front five can move; I'll be making this point, strongly, tomorrow and Saturday morning. One thing about this side: the harder the game, the greater the commitment they pour into it. We'll need all we can muster on Saturday.

We had a good practice today, concentrating on variations in the back play. Sometimes we'll move Simon Hodgkinson in to fly-half, pushing Rob to inside centre and me to outside centre with Jerry coming in from full back. That should disrupt their defence. If we can do it quickly at different times in the game they will have to improvise their defensive response, and I think we might find some weakness there. They're bound to be wary of the pace and running ability of our backline. We're going to change the emphasis: there won't be as many back-row moves from the pack as in last year's game. We'll vary the line-outs a lot more, using the shortened line which might have been useful at Murrayfield. More generally, we're looking to commit their defenders: to take the ball in to a man, to hit him and go to ground. Then we must move the ball away at once from the contact area, and have the rest of the pack sweep in so that the Scots cannot kill the ball. It's the quick ruck ball from these second and third phases that will produce the gaps for the threequarters to run into.

As another ploy, we're going to put kicks up and turn

them: Rob will be aiming at their wingers, forcing their back row to go backwards, rather than come flying up into the midfield and reproducing the pressure they put on Rob last year. The key will be to get our forward momentum going early on – to get the psychological edge there. Then they may give away a few penalties, and Simon will kick them. That's the plan.

It's ten to twelve now. Time to sleep and get ready for training at Bisham Abbey on the all-weather surface at eleven in the morning.

SATURDAY 16 FEBRUARY 1991

I'm looking out of my hotel window at Richmond, at 10.15 on the morning of the game – and it's a beautiful day. There's been a remarkable thawing-out over the last few days. Yesterday's training at Bisham went really well. The attitude seems to me just right.

The first five minutes will be crucial. Last year, we were shocked by the speed at which the Scots began. A lively opening will also help to get the crowd on our side; the support at Twickenham is getting better and better, and we want to make the most of that factor.

I took my usual walk last night. I went up the hill and got that wonderful view out over Twickenham, over the river and the silhouette of the stadium. I remember when I first went for a walk up there I had such a different outlook on the game: I was just thrilled to be playing for England. Now I've got twenty-two caps; and although I am still just as delighted to be playing for the country, that's no longer quite enough. We feel we are a really good side, and that to register that we've got to win the Grand Slam. This side is only going to stay together until the World Cup, or, if we are lucky, for the 1992 Championship. For Jeff Probyn, Wade Dooley and Paul Ackford, Mike Teague and Peter Winterbottom, time is running out. Because I've had so much fun with the team – and because I respect them as much as I do – I hope we can achieve something that we can savour together before the team dissolves. I think we know that to lose any game now would be the end of our aspirations: would be the end of us as a side. This is our last chance.

SATURDAY 16 FEBRUARY 1991, TWICKENHAM

ENGLAND 21   **SCOTLAND** 12

Try:	Heslop	**Penalties:**	Chalmers (4)
Conversion:	Hodgkinson		
Penalties:	Hodgkinson (5)		

England's new, no-frills approach stood them in good stead in a match which was constantly interrupted by referee Hilditch's obtrusive whistling. Early penalties gave England the lead, and thereafter complete line-out control allowed Andrew to keep the game pinned to the touchlines, while the Scots were forced to try to keep the ball alive even when kicking deep. Nigel Heslop scored his first try in internationals as England established a 15-6 advantage, and though Scotland, inspired by their tenacious scrum-half, Armstrong, clawed back to 15-12, England's grip on the game was never seriously threatened, and two more penalties by Hodgkinson sealed the outcome. The last few minutes saw a series of perfectly judged diagonal kicks by Andrew which had the frustrated Scots playing out the game in the shadow of their own goalposts.

ENGLAND: S. D. Hodgkinson (Nottingham); N. J. Heslop (Orrell), W. D. C. Carling (Harlequins) (*capt*), J. C. Guscott (Bath), R. Underwood (Leicester); C. R. Andrew (Wasps), R. J. Hill (Bath); J. Leonard (Harlequins), B. C. Moore (Harlequins), J. A. Probyn (Wasps), P. J. Ackford (Harlequins), W. A. Dooley (Preston Grasshoppers), M. C. Teague (Gloucester), P. J. Winterbottom (Harlequins), D. Richards (Leicester)

SCOTLAND: A. G. Hastings (Watsonians); A. G. Stanger (Hawick), S. Hastings (Watsonians), S. R. P. Lineen (Boroughmuir), A. Moore (Edinburgh Academicals); C. M. Chalmers (Melrose), G. Armstrong (Jedforest); D. M. B. Sole (Edinburgh Academicals) (*capt*), K. S. Milne (Heriot's F.P.), A. P. Burnell (London Scottish), C. A. Gray (Nottingham), D. F. Cronin (Bath), D. J. Turnbull (Hawick), J. Jeffrey (Kelso), D. B. White (London Scottish)

Referee: S. R. Hilditch (Ireland)

Other Match: IRELAND 21   WALES 21

SUNDAY 17 FEBRUARY 1991

That was one of the hardest and most exhausting games I've ever played in. Although the rhythm was a bit stop-and-start, the pace was frantic when the ball was in play, and the commitment on both sides was ferocious.

We knew that we had to start well, and we managed to exert good pressure in the first ten minutes, with a lot of impetus up front. Unfortunately, our tactical kicking wasn't as good as it should have been. All our first four kicks went too far, and allowed Gavin Hastings time to clear his lines with his celebrated big boot. If we could have put him under more pressure with two or three of those kicks, then we might have seen some spilled ball, and scrums in those tight situations might have produced earlier points.

The first half was pretty untidy, but the last penalty, just before half-time, was vital because we turned round with a 9–6 lead. Some people have said that Scott Hastings shouldn't have been penalised for what was a natural reaction: reaching out for the ball with one hand. I agree that it was hard on him, but the law states that unless you're going for the ball two-handed, as if for a definite interception, you're not allowed just to stick your hand out to block a pass. Anyway, it gave us that crucial kick.

At half-time we discussed how to improve our tactical kicks. We had to position them better, to put more pressure on Gavin Hastings and his wingers. Our back-row defence had been superb – really aggressive; but I wanted to put a little bit more pressure on them in midfield. Although they hadn't run the ball that often, we needed to clamp down on them there. I asked for a big effort in the early moments of the second half. We had noted that in each of the two games we had lost in the last two years of the Championship we had given a try away in the first minute or so of the second half. This time, we kept our concentration and scored a try ourselves. It came from just about the only bit of quick ball we were able to get. From the ruck, Rob fed inside to Dean Richards. Dean fed it inside to Peter Winterbottom – I went up on his shoulder and we managed to clear the bodies and Richard whipped it out to Rob, to

Jerry, to Simon, and Nigel Heslop was in at the corner.
The crowd were ecstatic. And that score was a tremendous
boost, especially as Simon kicked the conversion, because
it put us two scores ahead at 15–6. They did manage to
claw their way back to 15–12 with some dynamic play,
but once you are that far down in an international you
need luck as well as a massive effort to get back into it.
The cushion allowed us to take sensible, limited options in
the second half; and in the end we pulled away again
with two more penalties. The Scots were always looking
dangerous, but they were forced to attack from halfway,
or even from their own half, and that is a great compliment
to our forwards. A few of them had been aggravated by
the odd dig that they were past their best, and they
responded by winning clear victories in the scrum, where
we always had a nudge on, and the line-out. Wade and
Paul will obviously get a lot of praise for our touchline
dominance, but so should the props, who gave them such
good protection, and the back row, who sealed off the tail
so well. Behind the pack, Richard and Rob had things a
lot easier than Armstrong and Chalmers, but their tactical
kicking in the second half, especially Rob's, was superb. I
am sure it got to the Scottish forwards as the minutes ebbed
away to look up continually from a scrum or maul and see
the ball rolling into the corner thirty metres behind them.

And then there was Simon's place-kicking, which was
impeccable yet again. He's in the Grant Fox class by now
– there's no one better in the world. After Dusty Hare
retired, there were some England teams that would get
into good situations and force penalties which wouldn't be
kicked, and when they got no reward for their pressure
they would try too hard and errors would creep in. Not
any more. We know that Simon is going to kick the goals
if we win the decisions.

LINE-OUT DOMINANCE V SCOTS!

The referee, Mr Hilditch, has come in for a bit of criticism in this morning's papers. I did question some of his decisions early in the game, because I knew it was going to be close and I wanted to know exactly how he was reading things. A referee can't win, of course: you can't blow up for everything that happens in an international, and whatever offences you choose to punish, someone will accuse you of getting the balance wrong. From England's point of view I was not unhappy to see the game broken up as it was. The Scots may feel differently. There were areas of the game in

121

which I thought the referee could have been more consistent, but to accuse him of killing the game is to overstate things.

So now it's Ireland. In some ways this might be the hardest game for us this year, precisely because it's perceived in some quarters as the easiest. We will certainly be very strong favourites; Ireland will be dismissed lightly; and all the talk will be of a Grand Slam decider with the French at Twickenham. But the Irish in Dublin are nobody's pushover; and we have never been good at travelling as favourites. It is always hard to motivate yourself to the same pitch when you are regarded as the stronger team; when the cliché goes around that you can only beat yourselves. Well, we should have learned our lesson by now. For the last two years we have reached our last match as odds-on favourites, and we've lost to Wales in 1989 and then to Scotland last year. I hope this time we won't fall into the same trap.

I'm glad that Ireland scored such good tries against the Welsh yesterday (a 21–21 draw); we know now that they're capable of fluent, attacking rugby, and the media won't be so ready to write them off. I feel that as captain I am going to have to come up with a different angle on this game, something which will interest the players and spark a different approach from them. I don't really see the point in dragging out videos of the last time we lost to Ireland. That was back in 1987, when very few of us were involved. At the moment – uninspired as I am and still a little hungover – I see myself banging on about the lost chances of the last two years, but I hope by the end of the week to have come up with something sharper. In the meantime, there will be debate over the composition of the side, particularly if John Hall is fit and manages to play next weekend. I doubt whether there will be alterations in the backline; it depends how we view the relative fitness of players back from injury like Simon Halliday, but I think we can be fairly pleased with the play of each of the backs to date.

TUESDAY 19 FEBRUARY 1991

We're criticised in the papers today, I see, for not playing champagne rugby. Last year we played some great stuff, and got stick for being naive at the last hurdle; this year we have been very efficient and we get stick for lacking style. We just can't win. We don't play rugby to please the press, but it is galling when a particular sort of journalist, who predominantly covers football or writes feature articles, and who really knows very little about rugby, is suddenly lamenting the style in which England are succeeding.

In any case, it's not as if we've decided to play ten-man rugby this year because we want to win above all else. It's just the way the games have gone. We accept that we might have expanded a bit more against the Welsh, especially in the last twenty minutes; but when England hadn't won there for twenty-eight years, and we had such a weight of expectancy on our shoulders, we were just very anxious to maintain our advantage and get the game over successfully. There was an overcharged atmosphere before and during that game that wasn't really conducive to attractive play. And to win 25–6 was no mean achievement. It's the biggest defeat that England have ever inflicted on Wales, the biggest defeat they've ever suffered at the Arms Park. And how can anyone complain about the way we beat Scotland? Only a few months ago, in the Second Test of their summer tour, Scotland deserved to beat the All Blacks and very nearly did. They're superbly fit, highly motivated and very well-drilled. Their defence is excellent, and they manage to get around in numbers; I think one good try against that defence is a fair return. Two historic victories, and still there are sections of the English press who want to carp. When *will* they be satisfied?

FRIDAY 1 MARCH 1991, KILLINEY

Dublin is the away venue we look forward to most. As a smaller city, it gets completely overtaken for the weekend by an international; like Cardiff, but in a more kindly spirit.

We flew over yesterday after morning training in London, and drove out to our hotel, the Fitzpatrick Castle at Killiney, about half an hour south of the city. When we arrived there, the hotel staff were lining the steps to welcome us. We have three or four plain-clothes policemen with us wherever we go, and we're all staying on one floor of the hotel with a guard at either end of the corridor.

We trained today at the Blackrock College ground, where the ladies always put on a traditional tea for us of cakes and sandwiches. This year I made a little speech of thanks, and kissed them all – a pleasant part of the captain's duties. But I don't feel light-hearted at all about tomorrow's game.

Our preparation seems to have lacked an edge of purpose. We've found it hard to get a single idea to inspire us. Against Wales, we had our long sequence of failures at Cardiff; against Scotland, we had last year to avenge; and in the fourth game, if we win tomorrow, we'll be playing for the Grand Slam against France. But somehow we're lacking emotional incentive for this one, even though the Triple Crown is at stake. There's been an element of lethargy in our training sessions since Wednesday, and even in team meetings, that I've been trying hard with Dean and Rob to root out and eliminate.

And we'll have to be in the right frame of mind tomorrow, because I get the feeling that this Irish side is on the upsurge. They've got a new captain, Rob Saunders, who's full of confidence, half a dozen eager new players, and a new coach, Ciaran Fitzgerald, who's one of the most highly charged motivators in the game. They'll love being underdogs in Dublin against the English, and we can expect to see the return of the Irish fire of the early Eighties.

There's a French referee to worry about, too. They tend to shut their eyes at line-outs, which can degenerate into a free-for-all. Wade Dooley and Paul Ackford have to be ready for this; I'll call on them later on to see how they're shaping. If Wade takes the mickey out of me as usual, all will be well. A lot depends on him tomorrow.

My hope is that today's fine weather continues. Lansdowne Road is fairly soft underfoot already, and any more rain would suit their loose style of forward play, and prevent the expansive game we used so successfully against them last year. So – a nice, dry day please.

125

SATURDAY 2 MARCH: 10 A.M.

And it's pouring with rain and blowing a gale; it looks as though it's been raining most of the morning. The Irish will be rubbing their hands with glee at the prospect of a good muddy scrap, and we'll have to adapt our strategy. We might have the better side in theory, but these conditions will act as another leveller. At least none of the *team* think this is going to be easy.

SATURDAY 2 MARCH 1991, LANSDOWNE ROAD

IRELAND 7

Try: Geoghegan
Penalty: B. A. Smith

ENGLAND 16

Tries: Underwood
Teague
Conversion: Hodgkinson
Penalties: Hodgkinson (2)

126

Knocked out of their stride in a tense and error-strewn game, England were fortunate to salvage the Triple Crown (their first for eleven years). They took the lead for the first time through Rory Underwood's try with only seven minutes remaining. Ireland played with passion and flair, but they had cause to rue errors of judgement by their half backs: Smith twice kicked away an overlap. Simon Geoghegan, the discovery of the season on the Irish wing, scored a lovely try at the beginning of the second half, and for most of that period England struggled to turn possession into points against furious defence, in a way that became reminiscent of their failure at Murrayfield twelve months ago. In the last quarter of an hour, however, Dean Richards began to exert his massive influence, and he helped set up Underwood's try, the winger slipping through some uncharacteristically vague Irish tackles. Mike Teague's try in injury-time, from the base of a scrum, added a gloss to the scoreline that England scarcely deserved; and Simon Hodgkinson's conversion took him to an English record for the Championship of forty-eight points, though he had earlier missed four kicks out of six.

IRELAND: J. E. Staples (London Irish); S. P. Geoghegan (London Irish), B. J. Mullin (Blackrock College), D. M. Curtis (London Irish), K. D. Crossan (Instonians); B. A. Smith (Leicester), R. Saunders (London Irish) (*capt*); J. J. Fizgerald (Young Munster), S. J. Smith (Ballymena), D. C. Fizgerald (Lansdowne), B. J. Rigney (Greystones), N. J. P. Francis (Blackrock College), P. M. Matthews (Wanderers), G. F. Hamilton (N.I.F.C.), B. F. Robinson (Ballymena)

ENGLAND: S. D. Hodgkinson (Nottingham); N. J. Heslop (Orrell), W. D. C. Carling (Harlequins) (*capt*), J. C. Guscott (Bath), R. Underwood (Leicester); C. R. Andrew (Wasps), R. J. Hill (Bath); J. Leonard (Harlequins), B. C. Moore (Harlequins), J. A. Probyn (Wasps), P. J. Ackford (Harlequins),

W. A. Dooley (Preston Grasshoppers), M. C. Teague (Gloucester),
P. J. Winterbottom (Harlequins), D. Richards (Leicester)

Referee: A. Ceccon (France)

Other Match: FRANCE   36   WALES   3

MONDAY 4 MARCH 1991

The relief I felt when Rory touched down for his try –
when it seemed all might be slipping away from us again
– made it one of the best moments of my rugby life. I don't
suppose it was a particularly beautiful game to watch, but
I can assure everyone that to play in it was a really tough
test of patience and discipline.

We knew the Irish would be hard work in the rain, but
we were still surprised at just how well they played. There's
no getting away from the fact that we didn't manage to get
the control we wanted, despite the fact that we got off to
a good start and put pressure on them early on. Simon's
kicking was obviously less accurate than it has been. His
record is so remarkable that if he misses even a single kick
eyebrows are raised. Remember he's won us two games
with his concentration and his nerve, and it was just one
of those days where the ball just missed instead of going
over. One kick struck the post, and we didn't chase that
up nearly well enough. And then the Irish edged back into
the game, pressuring the offside line. We began to struggle

to control the ball when we had it. Our aim was to drive through the forwards, but frequently the ball seemed to spill or squirt out at the wrong time, and then the Irish would be on it, hoofing it fifty metres down the field. They were chasing as a team, and their tackling was really aggressive – until Rory's try.

There were one or two crucial turning-points in the game. One came quite early, when Ireland were 3–0 up; Brian Smith had another kick at goal. I remember standing under one post, watching it coming towards me, thinking how much harder it is to peg back a six-point deficit than a three-point gap. Anyway, the kick hit the crossbar and bounced down, and Rob – I think it was – scrambled it away. That was a big let-off for us. Then there were a couple of occasions when the Irish had overlaps and didn't use them; I think they'll be regretting those now.

In the first half we played into the wind, and at half-time I had to make sure we didn't relax just because the wind was going to be in our favour, as if the points were going to score themselves. Then, within two minutes of the restart, it was them, not us, who'd scored a try. This was the same point in the game that Scotland scored their try against us last year. I didn't want us to accept that that pattern could repeat itself. For about twenty minutes I had to concentrate on keeping positive, because we kept getting close, and then all of a sudden the ball would go loose again and Ireland would break out and suddenly we'd be back on our own twenty-two.

In such situations you start to get more and more frustrated, and more and more desperate, and you can feel this cramping sensation in your stomach, and a voice begins to say, *It's going to happen again.* But this time we won the mental battle, and kept plugging away until the points came. Maybe last year we would have let our desperation get the better of us; but this time, when Rob tried a drop goal and it didn't work, we eventually, sort of naturally, moved the ball. We hadn't tried it up to that point – and then we scored a try, with eight minutes left.

I've said we were forced to alter our game plan by the weather, and that was disappointing. But I think people underestimate how much preparation teams put in when they play England; Ireland had seen us running the ball round them last year, and decided that they'd got to stop us doing that. So not only the conditions but the opposition had a hand in the way we played. The other Home Countries might admit that they approach games against England with a special intensity and determination. When the Scots are playing the Irish or the Welsh, you often get open games with loads of tries – because both sides are more relaxed. But we're sometimes forced to play a more limited game by sides who are intent on disrupting our pattern rather than constructing their own. The Irish game was frustrating in that way; having said that, it's a Triple Crown, the first England have won for eleven years. Of course that's not nearly enough. We're not going to be satisfied if we lose to the French.

This side wants a Grand Slam. We've fallen at the final hurdle two years running, and we're determined to redeem ourselves. And from a Grand Slam point of view, it's a good job we were pushed so hard by the Irish. If we'd thrashed them and scored twenty, thirty points, on a dry day and in brilliant sunshine, we might have come away too pleased with ourselves, less prepared to raise our game one more notch, as we'll have to do against the French.

Dublin gave us a great night, as usual; win or lose, the city goes wild. We had our black-tie affair at the Shelbourne Hotel, then we drifted down Leeson Street to Strings nightclub, where they'd cordoned off an area for the teams. It was Guinness and champagne only, since Michael Kiernan and Paul Dean drank all the gin-and-tonic in 1989. When we got back to the hotel there was a band still playing, and Simon Halliday and Richard Hill took the mike with terrible results.

Alas, our flight back wasn't until four on Sunday afternoon, and at noon we were rounded up by Wade Dooley and company and forced to resume our drinking. This was especially bad news for me, as I'm not one of the stronger drinkers in the team, though I can keep pace with Rob Andrew any day; and it was quite a flight home.

SUNDAY 10 MARCH 1991

As you might expect, we're going to have an unchanged side for the French game. When you've played together for three internationals, it gives you that extra advantage of understanding, which is vital at this level: you begin to appreciate exactly which sort of line your partner in the centre or your winger is going to take. You don't have to spend that split second wondering what line he might prefer, or in another situation which foot he might come off. Soon your reactions to each other are instinctive. I think that might give us a little edge over France in a week's time.

Looking ahead at it now, with the game a week away, Serge Blanco is obviously going to want to make his mark;

this will be his last game in the Five Nations tournament. But that could weaken the French. His team-mates will want him to do well, and if we can stop him from running, and stem those magical counter-attacks, that might dispirit his whole side. I think we will focus a lot of our attention on making sure he doesn't get the room to move; and the same goes for the rest of their backs. We also want to move the ball around. Jerry, Rory and Nigel are the sort of runners who can cause anyone problems. Rory and Jerry certainly terrorised them last year. Nigel hasn't played the French at this level, but he's extremely elusive, he always beats the first tackler, and if we can let him have a run at Saint-André, who is a centre by instinct, on the French left wing, I think he might find out a weakness.

As usual this game is going to be won up front. The French always try to generate their forward motion from the tail of the line-out, from back-row moves; once they get over the gain line, Berbizier is an expert at just popping on. They will draw in the tacklers, and once they have an overlap the ball whistles down the backline. And they've done that beautifully for years. But if we manage to stop their back-row moves and line-out peels at source, and hit them behind the gain line, they'll struggle to generate any kind of momentum. That's our objective on Saturday.

WEDNESDAY 13 MARCH 1991

A calming interlude. I've just been in a flotation tank. I thought I'd give it a go, to help me relax before the game – they say the effects of your first one last two or three days. It's a big soundproof tank full of densely concentrated salt water at body temperature. You turn the light off when you get in, and you just float for an hour. It is one of the most relaxing things I've ever done. I'm sure I was asleep for most of it. When you get out you feel like a piece of jelly; you wobble around, and your mind is perfectly calm. I hope I wake up in time for Saturday.

Later in the day we had our first training session, which revealed an awful lot of pent-up aggression. I think we're all impatient – the next three days will be a long wait. We'll have to be careful that we don't come to the boil too quickly.

FRIDAY 15 MARCH 1991: EVENING

At tonight's final team meeting I went through the whole side, asking each of them what they thought was going to be their most significant contribution tomorrow. And then I added my own little thoughts on the areas where I think individuals have improved. It's a confidence-boosting exercise, telling each player what he is really good at; but I think it's been earned in all cases, and it might just give them a little extra spur before tomorrow. Most of them seemed to have focused effectively on tomorrow's priorities. The first of these is a solid set scrum. If Jason and Jeff can lock the scrum then we're going to get steady, quality ball. If we're being shunted even a little in the scrum then everything else immediately comes under pressure. Then we'd like to get the upper hand at the line-out. I don't think it's one of this French team's strengths, Roumat excepted. In defence, we must stop their runners on the wrong side of the gain line; its up to Rob and myself and Jerry to get those tackles in, along with the back row.

Strangely, I feel more confident for this game than for any of the other three. I don't know if it's because the French play a creative style of rugby, which we find easier to play against. Perhaps I've just got the anxiety out of my system. And it's reassuring that Les Peard is the referee. We've had him once before and I remember him as very fair and sympathetic. He'll see how the games going, make clear what he expects in each department, and go from there.

Well, whatever happens, this has been a good side – even if it lasts no longer than the World Cup. After that, I can see five or six of the squad deciding that enough is enough. As for tomorrow – I would just like to sit back in the changing room afterwards and not see the shared suffering we had after Scotland last year. I'd like to look up tomorrow afternoon at people who have the satisfaction of having achieved. I think we have done all the preparation we can. We've done our homework on the French. Tonight we had a final videotape put together by Andrew Davey – about five minutes, put to music, of our best moments, the big tackles, the tries, the best rucks – against the French for the last two years. It had quite an effect on the players.

A game like this – between two such strong sides – will be won and lost in a few moments of truth. If the ball goes our way, or if we manage to maintain our concentration in those moments, then we will win. If we let the concentration slip for a few seconds, or make basic errors at the wrong time, another Grand Slam will have slipped away.

It's going to be close. We rely on Simon to give us the boost of early points. We have proved against Ireland that we can come from behind, but I would certainly prefer to be ahead. Then it is just a question of maintaining concentration. The French are deadly when the opposition relaxes its grip. Now it is a question of each player working as hard as he can on his part of the team plan. If there are no lapses, I think we'll win.

SATURDAY 16 MARCH 1991, TWICKENHAM

ENGLAND 21

Try:	Underwood
Conversion:	Hodgkinson
Penalties:	Hodgkinson (4)
Drop goal:	Andrew

FRANCE 19

Tries:	Saint-André
	Camberabero
	Mesnel
Conversions:	Camberabero (2)
Penalty:	Camberabero

One of Twickenham's greatest days, with two fine sides of classically opposed styles – England's bludgeon against France's rapier – vying to be the unbeaten champions of Europe. England survived the shock of an extraordinary try, scored by the French out of nothing in the eleventh minute. Expecting the customary touch-down and drop-out, England turned away when Hodgkinson's penalty drifted wide of the French posts. Suddenly Blanco was running the ball across his own line and up to the twenty-five. Lafond and Sella handled before Camberabero cleared another defender with a brilliant chip and catch; then a cross-kick over the English cover, which Saint-André gathered to score between the posts. But England came back resolutely, three more penalties by the reliable Hodgkinson, supplemented by Andrew's snap drop goal and a converted

136

try by the ace finisher Underwood, giving them an 18-9 advantage at half time.

In the second half, control of the line-outs and a succession of forward drives kept England in the ascendancy, but the scores dried up, and France hit back with two late tries to set up a nail-biting climax. A last desperate attack foundered on England's twenty-five, and Les Peard blew his whistle on England's first Grand Slam in eleven years. Twickenham celebrated as it has never done before.

ENGLAND: S. D. Hodgkinson (Nottingham); N. J. Heslop (Orrell), W. D. C. Carling (Harlequins) (capt), J. C. Guscott (Bath), R. Underwood (Leicester); C. R. Andrew (Wasps), R. J. Hill (Bath); J. Leonard (Harlequins), B. C. Moore (Harlequins), J. A. Probyn (Wasps), P. J. Ackford (Harlequins), W. A. Dooley (Preston Grasshoppers), M. C. Teague (Gloucester), P. J. Winterbottom (Harlequins), D. Richards (Leicester)

FRANCE: S. Blanco (Biarritz) *(capt)*; J.-B. Lafond (Racing Club), P. Sella (Agen), F. Mesnel (Racing Club), P. Saint-André (Montferrand); D. Camberabero (Béziers), P. Berbizier (Agen); G. Lascubé (Agen), P. Marocco (Montferrand), P. Ondarts (Biarritz), M. Tachdjian (Racing Club), O. Roumat (Dax), X. Blond (Racing Club), L. Cabannes (Racing Club), A. Benazzi (Agen)

Rplacement: M. Cécillon (Bourgoin) for Tachdjian

Referee: L. Peard (Wales)

Other Match: SCOTLAND 28   IRELAND 25

SATURDAY 16 MARCH 1991:
6.30 P.M.

They've moved us from our Richmond hotel to the Hilton. I've been given a massive suite on the top floor with a magnificent view out over the city – there's Buckingham Palace down there. And I've got three bathrooms to myself. It's just as well we won, to justify all this extavagance.

It'll take a long time to come down from that game, and the reaction of the crowd, and the reception we got when we left the Rose Room. They had to cordon the whole area off so that we could get to the coach. There must have been a thousand people there, singing the new anthem: 'Swing Low, Sweet Chariot'. A lot of the players were moved by that: none of us had experienced anything like it. It was the first happy expression of the build-up of emotion that's been going on among English supporters. The Grand Slam means an awful lot to them. And as a player you feel privileged to have been a part of it; to have helped give the supporters all over the country something to celebrate.

There were some very tired bodies in the changing room a couple of hours ago. It wasn't a riot in there: but there was a lot of smiling and laughing and drinking, great relief and quiet joy bubbling around. No one had the energy to get up and shout about it. I don't know what this evening

THE GRAND SLAM!

is going to be like. I hope I manage to find my way back to my three bathrooms.

SUNDAY 17 MARCH 1991

What a game it was – especially given how much was at stake. The French scored three tries to our one, and they played some great open rugby, but I think the connoisseurs will have enjoyed our contribution too: technically we were the superior side, and we hardly made a mistake all afternoon.

Things were tight early on, but we were the ones getting in the decisive tackles. We also seemed to be getting the edge in the set scrums, where Jason Leonard was holding his own against Pascal Ondarts, who has a reputation as a troublemaker. A penalty kick from Simon had settled our nerves, and everything was going to plan when they scored that remarkable try. Obviously that took us by surprise, but we weren't too put out. The very fact that the try stemmed from moving the ball behind their own goal-line suggested that they weren't sure of the control they'd need to attack by more conventional means.

So when we gathered under the posts, I simply said: That was our own fault for not following up Simon's missed penalty in numbers. Now let's go back and get on with it. Rob dropped a goal almost immediately, then we kicked another penalty, and we were back in the lead at 9-6. By this stage we were getting the lion's share of possession, and the French were having to take more and more risks in their play to keep abreast of us. Then Rory scored a great try after Mike Teague's charge. An exchange of penalties, and we turned round at 18-9.

Now I knew we were going to win. Roumat was doing better than we'd expected against Wade in the middle of the line-out, but we had enough options with Paul Ackford at the front and Dean and Mike Teague at the back. And because of the efforts of our back row we were getting momentum in the loose and winning all the put-ins to the scrum: sixteen scrums to six was the final tally. With a platform of 18-9 and all that possession we should have put the game out of sight at the beginning of the second half, but we kept the ball a little too tight, probably through over-anxiety, and I think we began to look at the clock a bit.

Then they hit back at us with two tries, the second of them with only a few minutes to go. I still felt we were safe. We managed to pin them back in their own half for most of that final period, until the last few frantic moments. Ours has become a side that can maintain its confidence under extreme pressure, and strike back when it needs to. Still, with a few seconds left, they launched a last attack. Then I got hold of the ball near our twenty-five, and held on for dear life as the maul formed around me. And suddenly – with that wonderful blast from Les Peard's whistle – it was all over, and the crowd were all over the pitch, lifting us all on their shoulders.

It was marvellous, looking at the video today, to see the expressions of delight on Rory's face, on Wade's face and Peter Winterbottom's; after seven or more years of playing for England, this was their moment.

And mine too. I lost my boots to souvenir-hunters as they chaired me off, but I gained a satisfaction that will last for years to come. We got our Grand Slam. I know we didn't play the most flamboyant rugby you'll ever see; it wasn't *brilliant*; but it was very good. And it wasn't the French or the All Blacks – it was England.

THE GRAND SLAM
TEAM

Simon Hodgkinson [15] Full-back   (Nottingham)

A quiet man, he gets notably introverted, even nervous, before a game, but no one ever disturbs him when he's like that, as it's recognised and respected as part of his build-up. After the tension of a match is over, and when he's had a couple of beers, he's dramatically different, as anyone down at The Sun in Richmond will tell you.

Every great team needs an effective goalkicker, and right now there's no one in the world better than Simon, not even the All Blacks' Grant Fox. The total of seven penalties he kicked against Wales this year was a world record (until the Canadian Mark Wyatt surpassed it against Scotland in May), though he did it with his usual absence of fuss.

His place-kicking is his main value to the side, but his other strengths as a footballer have been underrated. He'd be the first to admit that he's not the quickest full-back around, but his spatial awareness and the sureness of his handling make up for that. You can rely on him to make the right decision when he comes into the line.

Nigel Heslop [14] Right Wing (Orrell)

When he was selected for the tour of Argentina, he would have been surprised to be told that he'd get capped out there, as Chris Oti and Tony Underwood were earmarked as the Test wings. But he showed a terrific willingness to learn and an eagerness to play out there, and that earned him the right to play in the Five Nations when other contenders fell away through injury or loss of form. It's taken him a little while to find his feet, as you'd expect; the Five Nations tournament is a very demanding experience, and Nigel had no time on the bench to acclimatise. But he's been a useful guy to have around. He'll always train hard and listen and contribute, and his sense of excitement communicates itself to guys who've been around for a few years and might have lost some of their own freshness.

He's a very elusive runner, who always beats the first tackler, and as he showed when bombarded by Gavin Hastings he's very secure under the high ball. After all his hard work, it was lovely to see him rewarded with a try against Scotland.

Jeremy Guscott [13] Outside centre (Bath)

Everyone always knew that he could run beautifully, dazzle opponents with his acceleration, and score scorching tries; but even when he came back from Australia as one of the heroes of the Lions tour, I was unsure whether he deserved selection over the all-round ability of Simon Halliday. This year, however, he's banished any doubts, and has become a world-class centre. Now he does the grafting work as well: he takes the ball into contact, he sets up rucks, and he tackles ferociously, as well as being one of the most dangerous runners in the game.

Jerry's great fun to be with, being a much more laid-back character than I am.

Will Carling [12] Inside centre   (Harlequins)

Rory Underwood [11] Left wing   (Leicester)

He's been an international player since 1984, which makes him by some way our most experienced back. In the Grand Slam decider this year he equalled Tony Neary's record number of caps for England (43), and he holds the record number of tries for an Englishman in internationals (now 27), and he's still only twenty-seven or so.

Rory stays tremendously fit without having to try too hard; he's got the enviable sort of metabolism that can absorb any number of hamburgers and not put on any weight. He's a committed family man with a baby daughter, and this makes him a calming influence within the squad. That said, you only had to see him jumping around when we won the Grand Slam to know what it meant to him.

Rory has always been a brilliant try-scorer, often from apparently unpromising situations. It used to be lamented that England sides never gave him the ball, but I think we've got round to using him properly in the last two or three seasons. In the same period he's tightened up his defence and cured a tendency to slip out of the game for long passages.

Rob Andrew [10] Fly-half   (Wasps)

Rob used to get such a lot of stick from the press, I was amazed that he still seemed to enjoy the game; and now he manages to deal smilingly with the press at all times. That tells you a lot about his attitude; he's very well-balanced.

Like Rory, he's got a baby daughter, and is in the first throes of a family life, which makes him very proud.

Tactically, Rob has been a great help to me; his calmness tends to keep my more emotional, intuitive approach in check. He takes the backs' meetings and leads us through our moves; his partnership and understanding with Richard Hill has been the lynchpin of our success over the last two years.

Rob is a great controller at fly-half, whether moving the ball or kicking for position. The highlights of his play this year were his kicking into the corners in the second half against Scotland, which broke their forwards' hearts, and the improvised kick along the right touchline which gave Rory his try against France.

Richard Hill [9] Scrum-half (Bath)

After being captain in the notorious Welsh match of 1987, he was dropped for two years; but he came back in the 1990 Championship to scotch the view that he was a little bit too volatile to be successful at the top level.

In his time in the wilderness, Richard improved his service as much as his attitude, and Rob has appreciated the extra time that has given him. His liaison between the forwards and the backs – and he has, unusually, earned the respect of both groups – has been a crucial element in our success.

Scrum-half has been a problem position for England since the days of Steve Smith, really; one or two players have gone out in the number 9 shirt who haven't really been international class. But Richard is the genuine article. He trains very hard and intently, throwing hundreds of passes a day, but that's dedication rather than obsession; and his temper is a thing of the past.

146

Dean Richards [8] Number 8 (Leicester)

A unique player, Dean was obviously badly missed when his shoulder injury kept him out of the 1990 Championship.

He is, of course, one of the strongest men in world rugby. He's also quite unorthodox, ignoring the conventions of Number 8 play, but he usually manages to turn up at the right place at the right time. He binds the forwards by example; as pack leader he doesn't say much, but when he speaks they listen. Very much his own man, he tends not to join the other forwards at the back of the coach, but prefers to sit on his own doing crosswords or reading; and he plays a lot of pool and cribbage with Jerry.

Dean has always had the Corinthian approach to rugby, especially to training. Serious preparation in the modern style doesn't appeal to him. It's quite hard to get him to take any theory too seriously – his copy of Geoff Cooke's motivational tape finished up, famously, in his bin – yet he manages to produce the most extraordinary performances on the field.

He has a tremendous will to win that transmits itself through the rest of the side. He sets extremely high standards for himself, and when he doesn't achieve them, he can be inconsolable, as he was after our victory over Wales this year, when he felt he'd played poorly.

Dean has kicked me once or twice when I've done the wrong thing, but in general he's looked after me brilliantly.

Peter Winterbottom [7] Open-side flanker (Harlequins)

Like Rory and Wade, he's been around a long time, and he seems to me now to be the complete player at number 7. People used to say that he had poor hands, but the last two

147

or three years, when he's been playing more sevens, have remedied that shortcoming.

He is one of the hardest tacklers in the game, as a lot of jittery midfield backs of the last ten years would testify. And you sense his strength off the pitch too; like Mike Teague, he's a quiet, hard man – almost shy, and happiest in the company of a few friends. He lives to play rugby, and isn't particularly interested in the public side of playing for England. The game's the thing for him, and he'll always give 100 per cent, however friendly the competition.

He's a great team man, completely honest and direct; if he doesn't like what you're up to, whether in your training methods or in selection, he'll tell you. I thought his reaction when we won the Grand Slam was terrific; it was great to see someone so quiet, who's been around for so long, get such excitement and fulfilment from one game.

Mike Teague [6] Blind-side flanker   (Gloucester)

Player of the Series as a blind-side flanker with the Lions in Australia, he then played through the 1990 Championship at Number 8, which is not his best position, only to be dropped for the Argentina game in December when Dean Richards became available again. An injury to John Hall gave him back his place at number 6, and he had a wonderful Five Nations Championship, with two tries as souvenirs.

Fiercely proud of playing for England, he's coped with the ups and downs that have beset his career with great strength of character. His response to the threat of his place last winter was to train harder than anyone else in the hope of getting it back. As a player, he's an unceasing grafter, with good ball skills too. He has a great relationship with Dean, and together they give us tremendous upper-body strength in our back row.

Mike has a good sense of humour, which is just as well, as he's often the butt of jokes from more boisterous team-mates. He doesn't pipe up much in team meetings or anywhere else, and prefers having a quiet drink with one or two of his fellow-forwards. On the other hand, he's very approachable, and easy to talk to, and once he's decided you're one of his mates he'll never let you down.

Wade Dooley [5] Lock   (Preston Grasshoppers)

Six foot eight, eighteen stone – quite a man.

He's hugely experienced, too, and he was one of those who, when I was made captain, might have looked at me and thought – Why should I listen to this flash little so-and-so with only a handful of caps? But Wade's always been very good to me, and these days I ring him up regularly for the sort of advice a senior forward can give. People look at the size of him and assume he must be a bit thick; in fact he's very astute. He's one of the quieter forwards, but he has a better sense of humour (of the northern variety) than his partner Paul Ackford; and although he doesn't often buy a round of drinks, it's always very much appreciated by the person he buys it for.

Wade started in international rugby in 1985, and he's had to make the adjustment to the new standards of fitness and training that have come into the game, which he's done uncomplainingly. One of the best second-rows in the world, he's a giant in the line-out, a powerhouse in the scrum, and a great deal more mobile in the loose than he's normally given credit for. He's very proud of what he's achieved, and quite rightly.

Paul Ackford [4] Lock (Harlequins)

'The Boss' burst on to the scene in a remarkable way. Although he appeared for England B in 1979 as a twenty-one-year-old, he seemed destined to play out his days as a nearly-man until he moved from Rosslyn Park to Harlequins late in his career. Suddenly he was playing for London; then for England (he got his first cap at the age of thirty late in 1988); then the British Lions. In the space of nine months, he'd come from nowhere to be the best front-jumper in the world; and the rise in England's fortunes has had a lot to do with the formidable partnership he's struck up with Wade.

Paul's a very intelligent man – he used to teach English at Dulwich College before he graduated to the police force – and he likes being involved in the planning stages. He's a natural leader, really, and does a lot of good work preparing the forwards. Paul likes talking, especially at mealtimes, when, if anyone dares to run a video he'll get up and turn it off.

His most conspicuous work on the pitch is done in the line-out, but he's extremely fit for his size and gets around the field very athletically.

Jeff Probyn [3] Tight-head prop (Wasps)

One of the most destructive scrummagers in the world. Though he's not particularly big for a tight-head, he is immensely strong and his technique is second to none. Equally valuable to England has been his clearing-up work in the line-out and the chores he carries out on the floor.

Jeff has always played his rugby for fun. Training has never been a passion with him, though he's now much fitter than he used to be. His fitness is quite an achievement when you consider that he lives in East London, where he runs

150

a reproduction furniture business, and he has to drive for hours to get to and from training sessions at the Wasps' ground in Richmond.

A late starter, he was first capped in 1988 when he was thirty-one. He's now thirty-five, and his mature outlook helps me to keep things in perspective. If I get too worked up about something, I can look up and see him smiling quietly to himself; there can, after all, be a funny side to playing for England. He does an annoying imitation of a telephone during team meetings.

Brian Moore [2] Hooker (Harlequins)

Player of the Year 1989–90. Fit, powerful and competitive, he's been the best hooker in Britain since he came through on the Lions' tour of Australia two years ago. He's technically very sound in the scrum, and an accurate thrower-in to the line-out, but I think his major strength is his work around the field, in loose and tight-loose situations, where he powers around dramatically.

There was a bit of speculation around last year about whether Brian was trying to take over my role, both on the field (against Scotland) and off, as spokesman for the players – but this was never the case. Brian is every bit as ambitious as the rest of us, and I think when I was made captain so young he couldn't see why certain senior players had been passed over. Ever since my appointment, however, I've always felt his wholehearted support, and we get on very well.

Brian does a lot of work off the field for rugby, especially for youth rugby; and belying his hard image on the field, he is absolutely devoted to his fiancée.

Jason Leonard [1] Loose-head prop (Harlequins)

Like Nigel Heslop, he won his first cap in the First Test against Argentina last summer, at the age of twenty-two – very young for a prop. But he has a mature head on his shoulders, and he has coped marvellously with the pressures of life in the international front row.

He's an East-Ender, born and brought up in Barking, where he played before he joined Saracens, and he brings a dose of Cockney wit into the changing room. Elocution lessons at the Harlequins have done nothing to change that.

Jason brings to his rugby, and to his fanatical training schedule, the single-mindedness of youth; rugby is literally all he wants to do. He's achieved so much in so little time that he seems destined to be one of the great forwards. He certainly has all the attributes; skill, hardness, the right approach. He's got thirteen years before he's as old as Jeff Probyn, so he could end up winning sixty or seventy caps.

Reserves

Jonathan Webb (Bath)

A doctor, he thinks things through meticulously, and is a valuable member of the squad. Moving to Bath had done him a lot of good – I think it's added a harder edge to his game. The way he's suppressed his disappointment at losing his place to Simon has been admirable.

Simon Halliday (Bath)

A wonderful player in the mould of the powerful, crash-ball centre, with loads of skill as well. His versatility makes him very useful to have on the bench, though it tells you something about our strength in the backs that he has to be there at all. Known as 'Cravat', partly for his habit of doing the *Telegraph* crossword on the morning of the game.

Dewi Morris   (Orrell)

Dewi has a great sense of fun, and is in permanent motion – his body as well as his mouth. He's always perking other people up, which makes him a great tourist. His dedication to the squad is demonstrated by all the help he's given Richard Hill, who's supplanted him in the team.

Paul Rendall   (Wasps)

His long-term partnership with Jeff Probyn had been inter-rupted but his capacity to adapt to being a reserve, and his enthusiasm for the reduced role, has been of great benefit to the squad. One of the funniest men in rugby, he's known as 'The Judge' because he presides over 'court sessions', and his humour is a great ice-breaker at team meetings. Like Dean, he comes from the Old School, and finds it difficult to suppress a grin at some of the new thinking that's come into the game – white-meat diets and all – but like Jeff Probyn his own fitness has come on a lot over the last couple of seasons.

John Olver   (Northampton)

Known as 'The Vermin', for his role as tour sneak – report-ing misdemeanours back to 'The Judge'. He got his cap against Argentina when they came here, but has spent an awful lot of time on the bench over the last two seasons. Even so, he's poured himself into squad sessions with total enthusiasm. He was my captain at Harlequins before he moved to Northampton, and has continued to feed me with useful advice. Like Dewi, he's always full of beans, and

leads the team ridiculing, as Mike Teague will tell you –
but always at the right time.

Mick Skinner   (Harlequins)

A proud Geordie, who's kept his accent, which we all hear
plenty of. One of the most lethal drinkers I've ever met.
Always involved in some prank or other, organising enter-
tainments, dress code and the rest. He has tremendous
energy on and off the field, and is always last in bed. That
said, he's worked extremely hard at his game, and he's
stayed utterly committed to the squad despite his limited
opportunities this year.

THE MANAGEMENT

Geoff Cooke   Manager

If any one man is responsible for England's Grand Slam –
and whatever else this England team might achieve – it's
Geoff Cooke. He had been very successful as team manager
of the North, but it was a mighty responsibility for him to
be made the first manager of England, at the start of the
1988 Championship. He took a long view from the start,
making it clear that his objective was the 1991 World Cup,
and that he wasn't going to chop and change in pursuit of
success in each year's Five Nations Championship; as an
example, I was allowed to mature into the captaincy in the
1989 season without feeling that too much was expected
of me. He identified his core of players and was obviously
going to stick with them, as long as they could show form;
and if he's had to drop anyone, he's always been frank to
the man involved. This sort of loyalty to the players has
made us loyal to him in return. When he came in for

criticism over the press boycott after the Cardiff match, we were behind him to a man.

The manager's job is highly complicated: Geoff has to liaise with the RFU, the selectors, the players and the media. The respect he gets from the press has been very valuable to me personally, taking a lot of the heat off. We do press conferences together, and I'm always glad of his coolness and judgement when the awkward questions start flying.

Roger Uttley Coach

Roger's main work is with the forwards. They're a close-knit group, and they give their respect grudgingly, but Roger's record as a 1980 Grand Slam forward and British Lion means they recognise him at once as one of them. If any of them have a problem they can take it to Roger and know he'll be able to empathise; and his international experience has made him a valuable figurehead in the management team.

As a coach, he has gauged the maturity of the players he's working with, and has allowed a high degree of independence, which the players have thrived on.

POSTSCRIPT
Preview of the World Cup 1991

WORLD CUP PREVIEW

Winning the Grand Slam has given great satisfaction, but it's fallen at a time when there's an even greater prize to go for straight away. The World Cup this autumn will be the most exciting time ever for rugby in Britain: and it would be wonderful if we could give the nation a triumph to match the 1966 soccer World Cup. And I think we can do it. Our preparation has been geared to this moment throughout, and for some of us the World Cup has taken on an immense personal importance. For at least half the pack it will be the last big event of their international careers. This England side, which has been through so much together, will inevitably begin to break up next winter. For myself, I first came into the England squad just after the last World Cup, and my appointment as captain always had this tournament as its long-term goal. And I know my career can never have another climax to match leading

England out to play New Zealand in the World Cup at Twickenham on 3 October – unless it were doing the same in the final four weeks later. It's thrilling, and daunting, to see the highpoint of your career marked out on the calendar, and getting closer and closer.

Assessing the opposition, there seem to be four other sides with realistic hopes of winning the competition. I'm discounting Wales, who must improve soon but are for the moment in serious disarray, and Ireland, who played some terrific rugby last season, but who have yet to find the habit of winning, and who have got to cope with the sudden defection to Rugby League of their fly-half and goalkicker, Brian Smith, and will have to re-jig their promising backline accordingly. So these are my teams to watch, in seeding order.

NEW ZEALAND

The World Cup holders, who've lost only once since 1986, will be odds-on favourites in most people's minds. And no doubt the old virtues will all be on display: phenomenal fitness, forward power with a ruthless streak, props who can handle and backs who can maul, Grant Fox kicking goals like an automaton, and a system of play that they've all been accustomed to since their teens. But I think there are signs that they are now more vulnerable than in recent years. Not only did they lose 21-9 to Australia in August

1990, but Scotland ran them terribly close – 18-21 – a few months earlier. And the balance of the side isn't what it was. John Gallagher's move to Rugby League has left Kieran Crowley at full-back a decent footballer but much less of a threat coming into the line. And in the back row, Michael Jones doesn't look quite the player he was before his serious injury, while at Number 8 Zinzan Brooke isn't in the class of a Mexted or a Shelford.

I don't think our backs suffer at all by comparison with their All Black counterparts. And we get to play them in the opening match of the tournament, when they'll have had only seven days to acclimatise. If we can beat them then, it'll give us a psychological edge if we get through to meet them again in the final.

AUSTRALIA

The Wallabies have managed to keep a low profile in the build-up to the World Cup, a surprise when you consider their recent defeat of the All Blacks. But our summer tour there showed us just how strong they are, and I place them only narrowly behind New Zealand as opponents to be respected. Their fitness is by now second to none, and they have the great advantage of drawing their side from two state teams only, New South Wales and Queensland, so their understanding will be very good. They will be strong in the tight, with any number of six-foot-seven locks to choose from, and have some potent strikers among their backs – notably David Campese. But most importantly they have the experience and tactical nous of Farr-Jones and Lynagh at half-back, who've played together since before the '87 World Cup. There's been a tendency to dismiss Australia as contenders since the Lions beat them on their own ground, but although they can be inconsistent they are capable of beating everybody.

FRANCE

France haven't had much success in recent seasons, but there are reasons to believe that they've turned the corner. They've installed new coaches, Daniel Dubroca and Jean Trillo, who seem to favour a much more balanced game than their predecessor Fouroux. Their backs, under the lead of Serge Blanco, have relished the return to traditional French style, and players like Camberabero, Lagisquet, Lafond and Sella can conjure tries out of nothing. But they seem to have an untimely vacancy at scrum-half.

Some of the new faces in the pack, like the prop Lascubé, and the Moroccan Benazzi and the very quick Cabannes in the back row, look like fine players. Olivier Roumat has developed into a top-class line-out performer, though the French still lack a competitive front-jumper. There's a good pack in the making here, but the World Cup may have come a year too soon for them. Our pack subdued them pretty well in the Championship, and I can't see them holding their own against the All Black front five.

SCOTLAND

The Scots have the great advantage of playing all their games at home up to the semi-final stage, and they're always very hard to beat at Murrayfield, which has become quite an intimidating venue for visiting sides. Ian McGeechan has built a highly-committed side who play a limited game to suit their own strengths, which are a really mobile pack and a wily, experienced back row, and a fast, aggressive midfield defence. Gary Armstrong and Craig Chalmers are maturing all the time, and Armstrong in particular has become a very awkward opponent.

But two weaknesses might undermine the Scots' Campaign. The first is that injuries to certain key players – to Sole, or Gray, or Armstrong – would expose their lack of reserve strength. The second is their lack of height in the line-out. They have to decide whether to experiment with a new jumper or persevere with their current combination and trust that they can get enough ball through ploys and variations. But I have a feeling that a coupling like Whetton and Jones or Dooley and Ackford could kill off Scottish aspirations at the touchline.

But England need fear no-one. We're going into this tournament with every belief in our own ability; our forwards and backs alike are as good as any of our rivals'. If we get it right against the All Blacks on the first day, the confidence that would give us might last all the way.

Enough speculation. The one sure thing about the World Cup is that it will be very, very exciting, for players and supporters alike. And since we're lucky enough to be playing, we're going to make sure, win or lose, that we don't let the supporters down.